DATE DUE

MAY 17 2007			
JAN 29 2008			
NOV 29 2012			

At Issue

Physician-Assisted Suicide

Other books in the At Issue series:

Antidepressants
Are America's Wealthy Too Powerful?
Are Conspiracy Theories Valid?
Are Privacy Rights Being Violated?
Child Sexual Abuse
Creationism Versus Evolution
Does Advertising Promote Substance Abuse?
Does Outsourcing Harm America?
Do Nuclear Weapons Pose a Serious Threat?
Drug Testing
The Ethics of Capital Punishment
The Ethics of Genetic Engineering
The Ethics of Human Cloning
Gay and Lesbian Families
Gay Marriage
Gene Therapy
How Can Domestic Violence Be Prevented?
How Does Religion Influence Politics?
Hurricane Katrina
Is American Society Too Materialistic?
Is the Mafia Still a Force in America?
Is Poverty a Serious Threat?
Legalizing Drugs
Prescription Drugs
Responding to the AIDS Epidemic
School Shootings
Steroids
What Causes Addiction?

Physician-Assisted Suicide

James H. Ondrey, Book Editor

GREENHAVEN PRESS
An imprint of Thomson Gale, a part of The Thomson Corporation

Detroit • New York • San Francisco • New Haven, Conn. • Waterville, Maine • London • Munich

Bonnie Szumski, *Publisher*
Helen Cothran, *Managing Editor*

For more information, contact:
Greenhaven Press
27500 Drake Rd.
Farmington Hills, MI 48331-3535
Or you can visit our Internet site at http://www.gale.com

Articles in Greenhaven Press anthologies are often edited for length to meet page requirements. In addition, original titles of these works are changed to clearly present the main thesis and to explicitly indicate the author's opinion. Every effort is made to ensure that Greenhaven Press accurately reflects the original intent of the authors. Every effort has been made to trace the owners of copyrighted material.

LIBRARY OF CONGRESS CATALOGING-IN-PUBLICATION DATA

Physician-assisted suicide / James H. Ondrey, book editor.
p. cm. -- (At issue)
Includes bibliographical references and index.
ISBN 0-7377-3245-8 (alk. paper) -- ISBN 0-7377-3246-6 (pbk. : alk. paper)
1. Assisted suicide--United States--Juvenile literature. 2. Assisted suicide--Juvenile literature. I. Ondrey, James H. 1948– II. Series: At issue (San Diego, Calif.)
R726.P4924 2006
179.7--dc22

2006016760

Printed in the United States of America
10 9 8 7 6 5 4 3 2 1

Contents

Introduction

The phrase *physician-assisted suicide* refers to the procedure whereby a physician provides the means for a patient to terminate his or her life, usually using a lethal dose of prescription drugs. The patient, not the doctor, is the one who administers the lethal medication. The person requesting physician-assisted suicide is typically a terminally ill individual who has decided to end his or her life without waiting for the disease to take its natural course. Patients seeking this option are motivated by a wish to forgo the prolonged pain, agony, and loss of personal dignity that accompany the culminating stages of a terminal illness.

Physician-assisted suicide is often characterized as euthanasia. Strictly speaking, however, physician-assisted suicide is distinct from euthanasia. Euthanasia is the deliberate killing of a person, usually in an attempt to end the person's suffering. A distinction is drawn between "active" and "passive" euthanasia. Active euthanasia requires an action that leads to the person's death, such as the administration of an intravenous drug. Passive euthanasia is simply the withdrawal of life-prolonging technology, allowing a dying person to die as the natural course of their condition. Active euthanasia can be either voluntary or involuntary; that is, done with or without the patient's consent. In the United States, active euthanasia—both voluntary and involuntary—is illegal, while passive euthanasia is legal and widely practiced.

Physician-assisted suicide is different from euthanasia in that rather than a physician or some other person doing the killing, the patient performs the act that leads to death. The doctor only supplies the means to bring about death. In the United States, physician-assisted suicide is currently legal only in the state of Oregon.

The issue of physician-assisted suicide has risen to the forefront of the nation's consciousness in recent years largely as a result of medical technology. The medical profession continually introduces improved diagnostic and treatment practices. Those who years ago would have quickly succumbed to their cancer, heart disease, or other terminal illness are now surviving longer. Advocates of physician-assisted suicide argue that this progress has not only lengthened the lives of terminally ill patients, it has prolonged their dying process, often leading to an excruciatingly slow, painful decline. For this reason, they contend, dying people should have the right to control the timing of their death and should be permitted to obtain a doctor's help in doing so.

Proponents and opponents make various arguments for and against physician-assisted suicide. Some of these deal with whether it is appropriate for doctors, who are supposed to heal people, to participate in bringing about the deaths of their patients. Others focus on the morality of taking a life—even one's own. Still others debate the potential societal consequences of legalizing physician-assisted suicide, with some fearing that it could lead to the acceptance of more extreme practices, such as involuntary euthanasia of disabled people. At the bottom of most arguments over the issue, however, are fundamental disagreements about the sanctity of life and the meaning of death.

Those who oppose physician-assisted suicide on religious grounds believe it is never acceptable to deliberately bring about the end of a human life. Life is a gift bestowed by God and therefore cannot be taken by anyone but God, according to these critics. In explaining why Christians must oppose physician-assisted suicide, Allen Verhey, a professor of religion at Hope College in Holland, Michigan, writes, "It is clear that God intends life and that God's cause is life, not death." Similarly, the Michigan Catholic Conference states, "Assisted suicide is a perversion of genuine mercy. . . . Suicide in any form prevents us from fulfilling the plan God intended for us when we were given life."

Some proponents of physician-assisted suicide counter this argument on the grounds of religious freedom. They insist that public policy regarding physician-assisted suicide should not be based on any particular group's religious views. This position was aptly stated by Bob Dent, the first person to legally commit physician-assisted suicide when Australia enacted a right-to-die law in 1996. Dent wrote that "the church and state must remain separate. What right has anyone because of their own religious faith . . . to demand that I behave according to their rules until some omniscient doctor decides that I must have had enough and increases my morphine until I die?"

Others reject the contention that physician-assisted suicide is necessarily a violation of religious tenets or of the sanctity of life. In an unusual divergence from traditional Christian thought on this issue, retired Episcopal bishop John Shelby Spong asks this pointed question, "When medical science shifts from expanding the length and quality of life and begins simply to postpone the reality of death, why are we not capable of saying that the sacredness of life is no longer being served?" He goes on to assert that "my deepest desire is always to choose death with dignity over a life that has become either hopelessly painful and dysfunctional or empty and devoid of all meaning."

Whether physician-assisted suicide violates the sanctity of life is among the issues debated in *At Issue: Physician-Assisted Suicide*. Throughout this anthology, authors grapple with the weighty issues that surround this timely topic.

1

Physician-Assisted Suicide Should Be Legalized

Sharon I. Fraser and James W. Walters

Sharon I. Fraser is a speech pathologist at Loma Linda University Medical Center in Southern California. James W. Walters is a professor of ethical studies at Loma Linda University.

The current debate over physician-assisted suicide concerns who will have the power to control the dying process—physicians or patients. A paternalistic medical profession must not continue to exercise the right to overrule a competent, terminally ill patient's decision to end his or her life. Criminalizing assisted suicide effectively nullifies the ability of terminally ill people to exercise the option of dying in a dignified manner. It is also an affront to the democratic principles of personal autonomy, justice, and the liberty to make one's own choices. Advocates of legalized physician-assisted suicide are not demanding the ability to dictate to society how one should die; they are simply seeking an option to make such a choice for themselves.

The first person to choose a statutory-sanctioned death with physician assistance was Bob Dent of Darwin, Northern Territory, Australia, who died September 22, 1996. This was possible under the Rights of the Terminally Ill Act, which had become effective in the Northern Territory July 1, 1996. By chance, one of us was in Australia and observed the resulting furor, which ran the gamut from approval to vociferous condemnation.

In particular, we were struck by a letter dictated by Bob Dent to his wife that outlined why he was making this choice and pleading that this "most compassionate legislation in the world be respected." He described an incontinent, pain-wracked, totally dependent existence that was exacerbated by watching the suffering of his wife as she cared for him. He was "immensely grateful" that he could end his life in a dignified and compassionate manner. In addition, he asserted:

> [T]he Church and State must remain separate. What right has anyone because of their own religious faith (to which I don't subscribe) to demand that I behave according to their rules until some omniscient doctor decides that I must have had enough and increases my morphine until I die?

In this article, we comment on some of the legal and ethical ramifications of this complex situation. Only physician-assisted death for competent, terminally ill persons will be discussed. Our society believes in the principles of individual autonomy, liberty, justice, and democracy. We consider that the interaction of the traditional value-of-life ethos, certain religious beliefs, and the stark realities of medicine at the end of life has most commonly resulted in an arbitrary "line in the sand" that is inconsistent with these principles.

The Legality of Physician-Assisted Death

Thirty-four states of the United States, including Washington and Oregon, have statutes explicitly criminalizing assisted suicide. Oregon, as the result of a citizen initiative ballot (Measure 16), has allowed a specific departure by permitting physician-assisted death under very restricted conditions. However, because of court challenges, initially no legally sanctioned physician-assisted death occurred. In May 1997, opponents of the law successfully persuaded the lower house of the Oregon Legislature to return Measure 16 to the voters for possible repeal. The principal opponents to Measure 16 are Physicians for Compassionate Care, whose leader is a devout Catholic.

In February 1997, the Ninth Circuit Federal appeals court upheld Measure 16 but allowed a stay to remain in effect until a ruling by the U.S. Supreme Court. The Supreme Court ruled in June 1997 (considering also a similar opinion rendered by the Second Circuit Federal appeals court) and effectively refused to grant Americans a constitutional "right to die." "However, their ruling did not preclude states from passing laws that would establish such a right: in fact, five of the nine justices suggested they might support such a claim in the future" [quoted from D. Savage, *Los Angeles Times*]. In November 1997, 60% of Oregon voters rejected the attempt to repeal Measure 16. The federal appeals court lifted the stay that barred implementation of the law. Both proponents and opponents of this "only one of its kind in the world" statute predict "the adoption of similar measures in other states" [according to K. Murphy, *Los Angeles Times*].

A report on the first 14 months of experience with the Oregon Death with Dignity Act draws some preliminary conclusions. Fifteen persons, 13 with cancer, have used the act [as of mid-2000] to end their lives, an estimated 0.2% of those eligible. Loss of autonomy and of control of bodily functions, rather than pain, were apparently the most frequent motivators. Unmarried patients were disproportionately represented; otherwise, demographic factors and education were not predictive. No obvious abuses of the law or unintended consequences have occurred so far.

In Australia, the Northern Territory legislation was short-lived. In March 1997, the federal parliament effectively repealed the "state" legislation by passing in the Australian senate the Euthanasia Laws Bill, commonly known as the "Andrews Bill" after its unapologetically doctrinaire architect. . . . Between September 1996 and March 1997, four competent terminally ill persons were able to exercise the right to physician-assisted death. Both the Oregon and Northern Territory laws had exhaustive provisions designed to safeguard the integrity of the legislation and prevent abuse.

Public Opinion Supports Assisted Suicide

Just how did society arrive at this impasse where we heatedly debate right-to-die legislation? In the past, most people died relatively quickly as a result of accident or illness. The rapid increase in medical knowledge, technology, and intervention often allows those who are terminally ill to linger. Despite the advances in palliative care, the death process is too often protracted, painful, and undignified.

Therefore, it is hardly surprising that in both the United States and Australia, public opinion polls have consistently supported physician-assisted death. In Oregon in a February 1997 poll, 61% answered "yes" to the question, "Shall the law allow terminally ill adult patients the voluntary informed choice to obtain a physician's prescription for drugs to end life?" An indication of social division even in Catholicism is that 50% of the Catholic voters answered "yes" to the same question.

Today, doctors are generally permitted to administer death-inducing medication, as long as they can point to a concomitant pain-relieving purpose.

Physicians' Attitudes Vary

It is difficult to generalize on physician opinion with regard to physician-assisted death. Investigation of current attitudes reveals a complex situation. Recently, the Oregon Medical Association changed its formerly neutral stance and specifically opposed Measure 16. This may be a reflection of the intense lobbying by the Physicians for Compassionate Care because previously two thirds or more of Oregon physicians surveyed favored a patient's right to obtain a physician's help in hastening death in certain circumstances.

In Australia, of 1,268 physicians on the New South Wales state register surveyed in 1994 by [P.] Baume and [E.] O'Malley, 59% answered "yes" and 3.3% "it depends" to a question [asking] whether they favored physician-assisted death. In 1995 Baume and colleagues looked at the question of religious affiliation and the practice of euthanasia and found that attitudes varied significantly according to religious affiliation, with "nontheists" most sympathetic. The "theists" who reported a Protestant affiliation were intermediate in their attitudes. Perhaps most interesting was that 18% of Catholic medical practitioners who responded recorded that they had taken active steps to bring about the death of patients when requested. In Michigan, the most important personal characteristic that defined physicians' views against "assisted suicide" was a strong religious affiliation.

Proponents Lay Out Key Principles

Whenever these issues are debated, certain terms keep appearing: "autonomy," "liberty," "justice," and "best interests." For a nonexpert to have any hope of understanding these terms, it is necessary to look at current medical reality. The Ninth Circuit Court of Appeals judges observed that "today, doctors are generally permitted to administer death-inducing medication, as long as they can point to a concomitant pain-relieving purpose." Physicians are aware that the medication may have a "double effect," a term that "originates in Roman Catholic moral theology, which holds that it is sometimes morally justifiable to cause evil in the pursuit of good" [as quoted from W. May, *Encyclopedia of Bioethics*].

The American Medical Association appears to subscribe to the euphemism of double effect with the following statement:

> The intent of palliative treatment is to relieve pain and suffering but the patient's death is a possible side effect of the

> treatment. It is ethically acceptable for a physician to gradually increase the appropriate medication for a patient, realizing that the medication may depress respiration and cause death.

Does double effect mean double standard? The debate seems to be about who gets to have input into decisions about death, and so far it appears to be the "omniscient doctor" referred to in Bob Dent's final letter. We can only consider a sampling or snapshot of an ethically and legally complex and confused situation but will nevertheless attempt to reach some understanding. Several ethical principles in our society bear on this discussion.

Liberty and Individual Autonomy

In the United States, autonomy or the principle of individual decision making is highly valued. The "liberty interest," a person's right of choice, is guaranteed in the Fourteenth Amendment to the United States Constitution. Thus, the issue of physician-assisted death is as much about control as about dying. Does a traditionally paternalistic medical profession continue to have the ability to override a competent, terminally ill patient's wishes and to insist on the right to "know best" in this crucial end-of-life decision? It appears contradictory that in the United States, at least, a competent, terminally ill patient has the right to make a legally binding advanced directive in anticipation of the inability to choose withdrawal of treatment (e.g. gastrostomy tubes) but is not permitted to hasten death by means of additional medication given with physician advice or assistance in the final stages of illness.

The Ninth Circuit Court judges were not impressed by the argument that physician-assisted suicide is different in kind, not degree. They drew an analogy between the withdrawal of a gastrostomy tube so that the patient starves to death and prescribing analgesics to relieve pain when these also depress respiration and result in the patient's death. In the former, the cause of death is starvation, and in the latter, the provision of analgesics. In neither case does the patient die of the underlying disease or injury. Addressing the issue of physician-assisted suicide, the judges stated:

> We see no ethical or constitutionally recognizable difference between a doctor's pulling the plug on a respirator and his prescribing drugs which will permit a terminally ill patient to end his own life. . . . To the extent that a difference exists, we conclude that it is one of degree and not one of kind.

These judges clearly recognized that some, perhaps many, physicians discreetly help their patients to die and acknowledge privately that this is so.

If autonomy is a highly valued principle, it is logical that patients, especially, and possibly family, should have the right to participate in all end-of-life decisions. Why should the most crucial end-of-life decision be arbitrarily barred? The criminalizing of physician-assisted suicide is effectively a prohibition of suicide for many terminally ill patients. The judges held that the liberty interest should allow competent, terminally ill patients the right to choose the time and manner of their death. They considered that adequately rigorous safeguards could be implemented in the decision process to prevent abuse. "We believe that the possibility of abuse . . . does not outweigh the liberty interest at issue."

How people die irrevocably influences how we remember them.

Justice and Equal Treatment

To most people, medical justice means the fair and equal treatment of patients. The current situation has elements of injustice. For instance, often competent, terminally ill patients are too debilitated to take active steps to end their suffering should they choose to do so. As it is an offense in most states for anyone to assist a suicide, many terminally ill patients are effectively denied private options available to those who are not terminally ill.

There is a perception that any change in the status quo will inevitably lead to widespread abuse. The rationale of this perception is hard to follow because those who hold this view have not demonstrated a necessary cause-and-effect relationship.

More than 20% of physicians in both the United States and Australia admit to taking deliberate action to end the lives of particular patients. This situation almost certainly disproportionately benefits more privileged persons in society because they are much more likely to have a relationship of trust with a medical practitioner who will discreetly alleviate their suffering. The former Northern Territory Chief Minister, when commenting on the demise of his legislation, observed that the senators who voted for repeal "belong to that privileged, wealthy group who have access to voluntary euthanasia themselves."

A democratic society that honors justice and liberty should . . . allow dying people a degree of freedom in when and how the end comes.

Family Autonomy

Another area that appears to contradict "best interests" is the effect of terminal illness on patients' families. First, how people die irrevocably influences how we remember them. Surely few would wish to be remembered or to remember a loved one as helpless, incontinent, pain-wracked, or sedated, as was graphically expressed in Bob Dent's final letter. Currently it is illegal to assist suicide in two thirds of the United States. Consequently, thinking people who are in unbearable pain die alone (if they commit suicide) because they do not want to put loved ones at risk.

For instance, a leading supporter of the Oregon Death with Dignity Act is prompted in part by the fact that his wife of 49 years committed suicide alone, which resulted in his subsequent investigation by the coroner and police. When they were considering the possibility of this kind of investigation, the Ninth Circuit Court judges observed that almost all who agreed to assist the dying avoided prosecution but would "likely suffer pain and guilt for the rest of their lives." Likewise, those who did not assist often question whether they should have tried to spare their loved ones. "This burden would be substantially alleviated if doctors were authorized to assist terminally ill persons to end their lives and to supervise and direct others in the implementation of that process." Indeed, physician-assisted suicide could prevent some premature suicides because patients would know that they had control over the time and manner of their death.

The Assisted Suicide Option Is Necessary

When the results of the vote in the Australian senate to repeal the Rights of the Terminally Ill Act were announced at 1 AM on March 24, 1997, the sponsoring senator hugged his wife, who was cradling their 3-week-old baby. This is a powerful image—the defeat of "death" in the presence of a new life. At such times, an image like this may influence thinking more powerfully than carefully reasoned argument.

Autonomous persons will not have uniform opinions. In particular, people will differ and change according to age, religion, and circumstance. A democratic society that honors justice and liberty should acknowledge and permit these divergent opinions and allow dying people a degree of freedom in when and how the end comes.

2

Physician-Assisted Suicide Should Not Be Legalized

Herbert Hendin

Herbert Hendin is a professor of psychiatry at New York Medical College and the medical director of the American Foundation for Suicide Prevention in New York City. He is the author of Seduced by Death: Doctors, Patients, and Assisted Suicide.

Legalizing physician-assisted suicide in the Netherlands and Oregon has not led to the compassionate care of patients. In the Netherlands, studies have shown that more than 50 percent of assisted suicide/euthanasia cases go unreported, and 25 percent of Dutch doctors have admitted to ending patients' lives without their consent. In Oregon, few safeguards exist to ensure that people are not needlessly put to death. For example, patients can receive assisted death without proving they are suffering intolerably and without undergoing a psychiatric evaluation. Rather than legalizing assisted suicide, governments should strive to expand the availability and practice of palliative care for their citizens.

Euthanasia is a word coined from Greek in the 17th century to refer to an easy, painless, happy death. In modern times, however, it has come to mean a physician's causing a patient's death by injection of a lethal dose of medication. In physician-assisted suicide, the physician prescribes the lethal dose, knowing the patient intends to end their life.

Herbert Hendin, "The Case Against Physician-Assisted Suicide: For the Right to End-of-Life Care," *Psychiatric Times*, vol. xxi, February 2004, Copyright 2004 by CMP Media LLC, 600 Community Drive, Manhasset, NY 11030, USA. Reproduced by permission.

Giving medicine to relieve suffering, even if it risks or causes death, is not assisted suicide or euthanasia, nor is withdrawing treatments that only prolong a painful dying process. Like the general public, many in the medical profession are not clear about these distinctions. Terms like assisted death or death with dignity blur these distinctions, implying that a special law is necessary to make such practices legal—in most countries they already are.

Assisted Suicide Arguments Are Weak

Compassion for suffering patients and respect for patient autonomy serve as the basis for the strongest arguments in favor of legalizing physician-assisted suicide. Compassion, however, is no guarantee against doing harm. A physician who does not know how to relieve a patient's suffering may compassionately, but inappropriately, agree to end the patient's life.

Guidelines established by the Dutch for the practice of assisted suicide and euthanasia were consistently violated and could not be enforced.

Patient autonomy is an illusion when physicians are not trained to assess and treat patient suffering. The choice for patients then becomes continued agony or a hastened death. Most physicians do not have such training. We have only recently recognized the need to train general physicians in palliative care, training that teaches them how to relieve the suffering of patients with serious, life-threatening illnesses. Studies show that the less physicians know about palliative care, the more they favor assisted suicide or euthanasia; the more they know, the less they favor it.

What happens to autonomy and compassion when assisted suicide and euthanasia are legally practiced? The Netherlands, the only country in which assisted suicide and euthanasia have had legal sanction for two decades, provides the best laboratory to help us evaluate what they mean in actuality. The Dutch experience served as a stimulus for an assisted-suicide law in Oregon—the one U.S. state to sanction it.

The Dutch Law Is a Failure

I was one of a few foreign researchers who had the opportunity to extensively study the situation in the Netherlands, discuss specific cases with leading Dutch practitioners and interview Dutch government-sponsored euthanasia researchers about their work. We all independently concluded that guidelines established by the Dutch for the practice of assisted suicide and euthanasia were consistently violated and could not be enforced. In the guidelines, a competent patient who has unrelievable suffering makes a voluntary request to a physician. The physician, before going forward, must consult with another physician and must report the case to the authorities.

Concern over charges of abuse led the Dutch government to undertake studies of the practice in 1990, 1995 and in 2001 in which physicians' anonymity was protected and they were given immunity for anything they revealed. Violations of the guidelines then became evident. Half of Dutch doctors feel free to suggest euthanasia to their patients, which compromises the voluntariness of the process. Fifty percent of cases were not reported, which made regulation impossible. The most alarming concern has been the documentation of several thousand cases a year in which patients who have not given their consent have their lives ended by physicians. A quarter of physicians stated that they "terminated the lives of patients without an explicit request" from the patient. Another third of the physicians could conceive of doing so.

Physicians Are Encouraged to End Lives

An illustration of a case presented to me as requiring euthanasia without consent involved a Dutch nun who was dying painfully of cancer. Her physician felt her religion prevented her from agreeing to euthanasia so he felt both justified and compassionate in ending her life without telling her he was doing so. Practicing assisted suicide and euthanasia appears to encourage physicians to think they know best who should live and who should die, an attitude that leads them to make such decisions without consulting patients—a practice that has no legal sanction in the Netherlands or anywhere else.

Compassion is not always involved. In one documented case, a patient with disseminated breast cancer who had rejected the possibility of euthanasia had her life ended because, in the physician's words: "It could have taken another week before she died. I just needed this bed."

Some Outrageous Examples

Since the government-sanctioned Dutch studies are primarily numerical and categorical, they do not examine the interaction of physicians, patients and families that determines the decision for euthanasia. Other studies conducted in the Netherlands have indicated how voluntariness is compromised, alternatives not presented and the criterion of unrelievable suffering bypassed. A few examples help to illustrate how this occurs:

Government-sanctioned studies suggest an erosion of medical standards in the care of terminally ill patients in the Netherlands.

A wife, who no longer wished to care for her sick, elderly husband, gave him a choice between euthanasia and admission to a home for the chronically ill. The man, afraid of being left to the mercy of strangers in an unfamiliar place, chose to have his life ended; the doctor although aware of the coercion, ended the man's life.

A healthy 50-year-old woman, who lost her son recently to cancer, refused treatment for her depression and said she would accept only help in dying. Her psychiatrist assisted in her suicide within four months of her son's death. He told me he had seen her for a number of sessions when she told him that if he did not help her she would kill herself without him. At that point, he did. He seemed on the one hand to be succumbing to emotional blackmail and on the other to be ignoring the fact that even without treatment, experience has shown that time alone was likely to have affected her wish to die.

Another Dutch physician, who was filmed ending the life of a patient recently diagnosed with amyotrophic lateral sclerosis, says of the patient, "I can give him the finest wheelchair there is, but in the end it is only a stopgap. He is going to die, and he knows it." That death may be years away but a physician with this attitude may not be able to present alternatives to this patient.

An Erosion of Standards

The government-sanctioned studies suggest an erosion of medical standards in the care of terminally ill patients in the Netherlands when 50% of Dutch cases of assisted suicide and euthanasia are not reported, more than 50% of Dutch doctors feel free to suggest euthanasia to their patients, and 25% admit to ending patients' lives without their consent.

Euthanasia, intended originally for the exceptional case, became an accepted way of dealing with serious or terminal illness in the Netherlands. In the process, palliative care became one of the casualties, while hospice care has lagged behind that of other countries. In testimony given before the British House of Lords, Zbigniew Zylicz, one of the few palliative care experts in the Netherlands, attributed Dutch deficiencies in palliative care to the easier alternative of euthanasia.

Palliative Care Is the Better Option

Acknowledging their deficiencies in end-of-life care, the Dutch government has made an effort to stimulate palliative care at six major medical centers throughout the country in the past five years in the hope of improving the care of dying patients. Simultaneously, initiatives for training professionals caring for terminally ill patients were undertaken. More than 100 hospices were also established.

Even if the Dutch experience suggests that engaging physicians in palliative care is harder when the easier option of euthanasia is available, for a significant number such training has become a welcome option. A number of physicians who received the training have publicly expressed their regrets over having previously euthanized patients because they had not known of any viable option. Such expressions of regret would have been inconceivable five years ago.

Developments of the last five years may be having a measurable effect. In contrast to a 20% increase in euthanasia cases from 1991 to 1995, the number of euthanasia cases in 2001 was no greater than in 1995. If education of Dutch doctors by palliative care instructors is successful, a gradual reduction in the number of cases of assisted suicide, euthanasia and involuntary euthanasia cases will be a measure of that success.

Oregon is experiencing many of the same problems as the Netherlands but is not doing nearly as much to combat them.

Oregon's Law Is No Better

Oregon is experiencing many of the same problems as the Netherlands but is not doing nearly as much to combat them. Although legalizing only assisted suicide and not euthanasia,

Oregon's law differs from the Dutch in one respect that virtually builds failure into the law.

Intolerable suffering that cannot be relieved is not a basic requirement for assisted suicide in Oregon as it still is in the Netherlands. Simply having a diagnosis of terminal illness with a prognosis of less than six months to live is considered a sufficient criterion. This shifts the focus from relieving the suffering of dying patients desperate enough to consider hastening death to meeting statutory requirements for assisted suicide. It encourages physicians to go through the motions of offering palliative care, providing serious psychiatric consultation or making an effort to protect those vulnerable to coercion.

In Oregon, when a terminally ill patient makes a request for assisted suicide, physicians are required to point out that palliative care and hospice care are feasible alternatives. They are not required, however, to be knowledgeable about how to relieve either physical or emotional suffering in terminally ill patients. Without such knowledge, the physician cannot present feasible alternatives. Nor are physicians who lack this knowledge required to refer any patient requesting assisted suicide for consultation with a physician knowledgeable about palliative care.

The inadequacy of palliative care consultation in Oregon was underscored by a survey of Oregon physicians who received the first 142 requests for assisted suicide since the law went into effect. In only 13% of cases was a palliative care consultation recommended, and we do not know how many of these recommendations were actually implemented.

Compromising the Offer of Palliative Care

Two Oregon cases illustrate how compromised the offer of palliative care can become. The first patient, referred to by her physician as "Helen," was the first known case of physician-assisted suicide in the state. The case was publicized by the

Compassion in Dying Federation, an advocacy organization for physician-assisted suicide.

Helen, an Oregon woman in her mid-80s, had metastatic breast cancer and was in a home-hospice program. Her physician had not been willing to assist in her suicide for reasons that were not specified and a second physician refused on the grounds that she was depressed.

Patients who desire an early death during a serious or terminal illness are usually suffering from a treatable depressive condition.

Helen called Compassion in Dying and was referred to a physician who would assist her. After her death, a Compassion in Dying press conference featured a taped interview said to have been made with Helen two days before her death. In it, the physician tells her that it is important she understand that there are other choices she could make that he will list for her—which he does in only three sentences covering hospice support, chemotherapy and hormonal therapy.

> Doctor: There is, of course, all sorts of hospice support that is available to you. There is, of course, chemotherapy that is available that may or may not have any effect, not in curing your cancer, but perhaps in lengthening your life to some extent. And there is also available a hormone which you were offered before by the oncologist, tamoxifen, which is not really chemotherapy but would have some possibility of slowing or stopping the course of the disease for some period of time.
>
> Helen: Yes, I don't want to take that.
>
> Doctor: All right, OK, that's pretty much what you need to understand.

Psychiatric Evaluations Should Be Required

A cursory, dismissive presentation of alternatives precludes any autonomous decision by the patient. Autonomy is further compromised by the failure to mandate psychiatric evaluation. Such an evaluation is the standard of care for patients who are suicidal, but the Oregon law does not require it in cases of assisted suicide.

Physicians must refer patients to licensed psychiatrists or psychologists only if they believe the patients' judgment is impaired. A diagnosis of depression per se is not considered a sufficient reason for such a referral. However, as with other individuals who are suicidal, patients who desire an early death during a serious or terminal illness are usually suffering from a treatable depressive condition. In any case, studies have also shown that non-psychiatric physicians are not reliably able to diagnose depression, let alone to determine whether the depression is impairing judgment.

Not all of the factors justifying a psychiatric consultation center on current depression. Patients requesting a physician's assistance in suicide are usually telling us that they desperately need relief from their mental and physical suffering and that without such relief they would rather die. When they are treated by a physician who can hear their desperation, understand their ambivalence, treat their depression and relieve their suffering, their wish to die usually disappears.

Protecting Doctors, Not Patients

The psychiatric consultation as envisioned by the Oregon law is not intended to deal with these considerations. It is only concerned with the more limited issue of a patient's capacity to make the decision for assisted suicide to satisfy the requirement of informed consent. The story of Joan Lucas, whose suicide was also facilitated and publicized by Compassion in Dying, points out how such a gatekeeper role encourages seeking psychological or psychiatric consultation to protect doctors, rather than patients.

Lucas, an Oregon patient with amyotrophic lateral sclerosis, attempted suicide. Paramedics were called to her house, but her children sent them away, explaining, "We couldn't let her go to the ambulance. They would have resuscitated her."

Lucas survived her attempt and was assisted in suicide 18 days later by a physician who gave interviews about the case to an Oregon newspaper on condition of anonymity. He stated that after talking with attorneys and agreeing to help aid Lucas in her death, he asked her to undergo a psychological examination. "It was an option for us to get a psychological or psychiatric evaluation," he told the newspaper. "I elected to get a psychological evaluation because I wished to cover my ass. I didn't want there to be any problems."

The doctor and the family found a cooperative psychologist who asked Lucas to take the Minnesota Multiphasic Personality Inventory (MMPI). Because it was difficult for Joan to travel to the psychologist's office, her children read the true-false questions to her at home. The family found the questions funny, and Joan's daughter described the family as "cracking up over them." Based on these test results, the psychologist concluded that whatever depression Joan had was directly related to her terminal illness—a completely normal response. His opinion is suspect, the more so because while he was willing to give an opinion that would facilitate ending Joan's life, he did not feel it was necessary to see her first.

Inadequacy of End-of-Life Care

Data from patient interviews, surveys of families of patients receiving end-of-life care in Oregon, surveys of physicians' experience and data from the few cases where information has been made available suggest the inadequacy of end-of-life care in Oregon.

Oregon physicians have been given authority without being in a position to exercise it responsibly. They are expected to inform patients that alternatives are possible without being required to be knowledgeable enough to present those alternatives in a meaningful way, or to consult with someone who is. They are expected to evaluate patient decision-making capacity and judgment without a requirement for psychiatric expertise or consultation. They are expected to make decisions about voluntariness without having to see those close to the patient who may be exerting a variety of pressures, from subtle to coercive. They are expected to do all of this without necessarily knowing the patient for longer than 15 days. Since physicians cannot be held responsible for wrongful deaths if they have acted in good faith, substandard medical practice is encouraged, physicians are protected from the consequences, and patients are left unprotected while believing they have acquired a new right.

The World Health Organization has recommended that governments not consider assisted suicide and euthanasia until they have demonstrated the availability and practice of palliative care for their citizens. All states and all countries have a long way to go to achieve this goal.

People are only beginning to learn that with well-trained doctors and nurses and good end-of-life care, it is possible to avoid the pain of the past experiences of many of their loved ones and to achieve a good death. The right to such care is the right that patients should demand and the challenge that every country needs to meet.

3

The Supreme Court Was Right to Uphold Oregon's Assisted-Suicide Law

E.J. Dionne

E.J. Dionne is a nationally syndicated columnist with the Washington Post Writers Group. He specializes in analyzing the strengths and weaknesses of current American political philosophies.

The Supreme Court was correct to uphold Oregon's Death with Dignity Act, which allows physicians to assist terminally ill people to commit suicide. Although assisted suicide is morally questionable, states should be free to decide the issue for themselves. The Oregon law was passed by the state's voters and was reconfirmed in a repeal election. The executive branch's attempt to overturn the law was an excessive use of federal power that threatened the right of states to regulate their own medical practices. The Supreme Court acted appropriately when it checked this unconstitutional action.

I believe that legalizing physician-assisted suicide is a mistake. I also believe that having federal courts and bureaucrats decide the issue is a mistake. This is a question that should be debated by the people and their representatives.

That's why the Supreme Court was right . . . to uphold Oregon's assisted-suicide law—a law I would have voted against had I been an Oregon citizen, and would vote to repeal.

E.J. Dionne, "High Court Ruling on Assisted Suicide; Letting the People Decide," *The Record*, January 20, 2006, p. L09.

Oregon passed the law in a referendum. Six justices on the Supreme Court rejected sweeping claims by the [George W.] Bush administration (originally put forward by former Attorney General John Ashcroft) that it could interpret federal laws in a novel way to usurp Oregon's power to regulate the practice of medicine. This, Justice Anthony Kennedy declared, represented a "radical shift of authority from the states to the federal government."

In this case, I found myself in the odd position of agreeing with the sentiments expressed by Justice Antonin Scalia on the underlying issue, but bewildered by his willingness to impose his view (and mine) by judicial fiat.

The Dissenting Opinion Was Weak

In his dissent, joined by Chief Justice John Roberts and Justice Clarence Thomas, Scalia relied on the vast constitutional authority of—Webster's dictionary.

Scalia cited Webster's to back up the following claim: "Virtually every relevant source of authoritative meaning confirms that the phrase 'legitimate medical purpose' does not include intentionally assisting suicide. 'Medicine' refers to '(t)he science and art dealing with the prevention, cure or alleviation of disease.'"

As a policy matter, I agree with Scalia that the problem with physician-assisted suicide is that it dangerously muddles the moral role of the doctor. To put it as plainly as possible: I do not think doctors should have the right to help people kill themselves.

Assisted suicide is the wrong answer to the right questions. Should the medical profession do a far better job alleviating the pain of those suffering from terminal illnesses? Should our high-tech medical system do as much as it can to allow people to die with dignity? Obviously, yes. But so far—happily, I would argue—most states have tried to solve these problems through measures short of assisted suicide.

But Scalia, Roberts and Thomas would claim the right to impose this view on Oregon. As Scalia himself writes, the legitimacy of physician-assisted suicide "ultimately rests, not on 'science' or 'medicine,' but on a naked value judgment."

The majority [Supreme Court opinion] does not try to judge the question of assisted suicide. It would keep open the public's right to debate this genuinely difficult issue....

Yes, and why should Ashcroft and the Bush administration be able to cast aside the decision of Oregon's voters and insist upon their own "naked value judgement"? Isn't it strange that those who typically advocate for states' rights—including, for reasons I respect, on the abortion question—then turn around and endorse the most expansive use of federal power to advance their own preferences?

The Majority Opinion Was Balanced

By contrast to the conservative judicial activism of the dissenters, Kennedy's majority decision is a model of judicial modesty. The court's majority takes a careful look at the language of the Controlled Substances Act. It finds no warrant for what it sees as the "unrestrained" power that Ashcroft was claiming in using the law to prohibit doctors from prescribing drugs in assisted-suicide cases.

The majority does not try to judge the question of assisted suicide. It would keep open the public's right to debate this genuinely difficult issue.

It cannot have been lost on senators about to vote on Judge Samuel Alito's nomination that the recently confirmed Roberts, for all his charming and intelligent talk about judicial restraint at his Senate hearings, cast his first dissent with the court's most activist conservatives.

In his own hearings, Alito would not even go as far as Roberts did in claiming to believe in modesty on the part of judges.

For the life of me, I cannot understand why moderates in both political parties do not see that Alito's confirmation would continue to push the court toward an activist jurisprudence determined to write conservative ideological preferences into law. [*Editor's note:* Alito was confirmed in January 2006.]

President Bush surely knew what he was doing when he named Roberts and then Alito to the court.

Bush and his conservative allies have the guts to fight for the future they want. You wonder if those with a different vision can show the same determination.

As it happens, assisted suicide is one issue on which my beliefs coincide with those of many conservatives.

But I want my view to prevail through persuasion in the democratic process, not because an attorney general and sympathetic judges impose it on every state in the union.

4

The Supreme Court's Assisted-Suicide Ruling Will Have Little Impact

Wesley J. Smith

Wesley J. Smith is a senior fellow at the Discovery Institute of Seattle, Washington; an attorney and a consultant for the International Task Force on Euthanasia and Assisted Suicide; and a special consultant to the Center for Bioethics and Culture. His books include Forced Exit: The Slippery Slope from Assisted Suicide to Legalized Murder, Culture of Death: The Assault on Medical Ethics in America, *and* Consumer's Guide to a Brave New World.

The U.S. Supreme Court's ruling upholding Oregon's Death with Dignity Act, a law that permits physician-assisted suicide in that state, was disappointing. The media, however, have exaggerated the significance of the ruling. The opinion was not a sweeping endorsement of physician-assisted suicide. The mildly written opinion will generate little interest beyond readers of law reviews and will do little to revitalize the movement to legalize physician-assisted suicide.

The news about [the Supreme Court's] 6-3 assisted suicide ruling is not as bad as euthanasia opponents might have feared. Indeed, even in the midst of disappointment that Oregon carried the day, there is some moderately good news: *Gonzales v. Oregon* was not an exercise in judicial activism.

Wesley J. Smith, "Nothing to Die Over," www.nationalreview.com, January 18, 2006. Reproduced by permission.

The Supreme Court did not issue a sweeping endorsement of physician-assisted suicide. Nor, did it "uphold" the Oregon statue as a matter of constitutional law. Rather, the Court's decision is so narrowly drawn and steeped in the arcana of regulatory and statutory interpretation that it would normally spark little interest outside of administrative-law journals.

Of course, that isn't a storyline likely to sell newspapers. Hence, the general media spin about the case has been that, as [wire service] Reuters put it, the Supremes issued a "stinging rebuke" to the administration and endorsed assisted suicide as a legitimate public policy. But this isn't true. Justice Anthony Kennedy's majority decision even acknowledged that the Justice Department was "reasonable" in its assertion that "medicine's boundaries" preclude assisted suicide. The majority also explicitly agreed that the federal government possesses the inherent power to prevent narcotics from being prescribed for assisted suicide, for example, by amending the federal Controlled Substances Act [CSA]. The case provided neither a sweeping assertion of the validity of assisted suicide nor a ringing endorsement of its legality being strictly a matter of state's rights.

The Court's Ruling Was Arcane

So if the federal government can, in theory, preclude controlled substances from being used in assisted suicide, why did it lose? The majority believed that former Attorney General John Ashcroft went about that task in the wrong way. Specifically, it ruled that Ashcroft exceeded his authority when he determined that assisted suicide was not a "legitimate medical use" of controlled substances without obtaining any information about the practice of medicine, assisted suicide, or other relevant matters necessary to come to that conclusion from outside the Department of Justice. Consequently, the Court found, Ashcroft's interpretation, while reasonable, was not persuasive because it exceeded his "expertise."

Instead of the Department of Justice, the proper place to determine the medical (il)legitimacy of assisted suicide lies elsewhere within the executive bureaucracy (presumably the Department of Health and Human Services) where bureaucrats and management would possess greater depth of knowledge about medical issues. (I told you the ruling was mind-numbingly arcane.)

Finally, the Court interpreted the Controlled Substances Act as primarily aimed at controlling drug trafficking and addiction. Hence, Justice Kennedy wrote that it cannot be read to explicitly preclude assisted suicide. And it is true: The CSA is silent about assisted suicide—probably because when it was passed decades ago, lawmakers never dreamed that it would ever be an issue. Recent legislative efforts to outlaw the use of controlled substances for assisted suicide, while promoting their aggressive use in pain control, foundered on the shoals of a Senate filibuster led by Oregon Democrat Senator Ron Wyden.

A recent Pew Poll found that support and opposition to assisted suicide was evenly divided 46 percent for and 45 percent against—hardly an unstoppable political tide.

Dissenting Opinions Were on Point

The dissenting opinions were first rate. Justice Antonin Scalia (joined by Chief Justice John Roberts and Justice Clarence Thomas) complained that "if the term 'legitimate medical purpose' has any meaning, it surely excludes the prescription of drugs to produce death." Scalia seemed to be hinting that the majority refused to enforce this commonsense and admittedly "reasonable" finding because its ruling was result-driven rather than legally mandated. Justice Thomas's individual dissent supported this view when he noted that the Court's reasoning directly contradicted its own seven-month-old ruling in *Gonzales v. Raich*—a medical-marijuana case. "The Court's reliance upon the constitutional principles it rejected in *Raich*," Thomas sarcastically noted, "is perplexing."

But that is all grist for law-review articles and legal symposia. The real question is what the likely political impact of the decision will be—or, more accurately stated, the effect likely to be produced by the spin about the case that will be produced by the media and assisted-suicide advocates.

Public Opinion Is Still Evenly Divided

There seems little doubt that the ruling will put some wind back into the sails of the assisted-suicide/euthanasia movement that has been becalmed in the United States for the last decade. But it will be a slight breeze, not a gale. In truth, legalizing assisted suicide is very low on people's political-priority scale. Demonstrators are not exactly marching in the streets demanding the right to be killed by a doctor, and few politicians run on the plank of authorizing physicians to write lethal drug prescriptions. Indeed, a recent Pew Poll found that support and opposition to assisted suicide was evenly divided 46 percent for and 45 percent against—hardly an unstoppable political tide. Moreover, experience has shown that when people are forced to look beyond the abstract idea of assisted suicide and actively consider the dysfunctional real-world *context* in which assisted suicide would be practiced—the problems associated with HMOs [health maintenance organizations], difficulties in obtaining quality health insurance, and rampant elder abuse, to mention just a few—their support for transforming killing into a medical act sinks like a crowbar thrown off of a bridge.

The American euthanasia movement has not moved its agenda forward since 1994 when Oregon legalized assisted suicide. Beyond relatively small cadres of very dedicated activists, both pro and con, most people are just not that interested in the issue. Thus, the limited ruling issued by the Supreme Court . . . is unlikely to have a sufficiently substantive impact to materially change the current political dynamic.

5

Hastening Death Is Contrary to Christian Beliefs

John Paul II

Pope John Paul II led the Roman Catholic Church from October 1978 until his death in April 2005—one of the longest pontificates in the history of the church. His books include Roman Triptych; Arise, Let Us Be Going; *and* Memory and Identity.

The human quality of those who are in the clinical condition called the vegetative state is not diminished by their affliction. In God's eyes, they continue to retain their value and human dignity in all of its fullness. As such, they still have the right to basic health and rehabilitative care. To hasten their death by withdrawing nutrition and hydration is immoral and a serious violation of God's law.

Editor's note: This viewpoint is taken from John Paul II's address to the International Congress on Life-Sustaining Treatments and Vegetative State: Scientific Advances and Ethical Dilemmas in 2004.

This important Congress, organized jointly by the Pontifical Academy for Life and the International Federation of Catholic Medical Associations, is dealing with a very significant issue: *the clinical condition called the "vegetative state"*. The complex scientific, ethical, social and pastoral implications of such a condition require in-depth reflections and a fruitful interdisciplinary dialogue. . . .

John Paul II, "Address to Participants in the International Congress on 'Life-Sustaining Treatments and Vegetative State: Scientific Advances and Ethical Dilemmas'," www.vatican.ca, March 20, 2004. Reproduced by permission.

Treating Persons in a Vegetative State

With deep esteem and sincere hope, the Church encourages the efforts of men and women of science who, sometimes at great sacrifice, daily dedicate their task of study and research to the improvement of the diagnostic, therapeutic, prognostic and rehabilitative possibilities confronting those patients who rely completely on those who care for and assist them. The person in a vegetative state, in fact, shows no evident sign of self-awareness or of awareness of the environment, and seems unable to interact with others or to react to specific stimuli.

Medical science . . . is still unable to predict with certainty who among patients in [a vegetative state] will recover and who will not.

Scientists and researchers realize that one must, first of all, arrive at a correct diagnosis, which usually requires prolonged and careful observation in specialized centres, given also the high number of diagnostic errors reported in the literature. Moreover, not a few of these persons, with appropriate treatment and with specific rehabilitation programmes, have been able to emerge from a vegetative state. On the contrary, many others unfortunately remain prisoners of their condition even for long stretches of time and without needing technological support.

In particular, the term *permanent vegetative state* has been coined to indicate the condition of those patients whose "vegetative state" continues for over a year. Actually, there is no different diagnosis that corresponds to such a definition, but only a conventional prognostic judgment, relative to the fact that the recovery of patients, statistically speaking, is ever more difficult as the condition of vegetative state is prolonged in time.

Even in Illness, Our Human Quality Persists

However, we must neither forget nor underestimate that there are well-documented cases of at least partial recovery even after many years; we can thus state that medical science, up until now, is still unable to predict with certainty who among patients in this condition will recover and who will not.

> *Our brothers and sisters who find themselves in . . . a 'vegetative state' retain their human dignity in all its fullness.*

Faced with patients in similar clinical conditions, there are some who cast doubt on the persistence of the "human quality" itself, almost as if the adjective "vegetative" (whose use is now solidly established), which symbolically describes a clinical state, could or should be instead applied to the sick as such, actually demeaning their value and personal dignity. In this sense, it must be noted that this term, even when confined to the clinical context, is certainly not the most felicitous when applied to human beings.

In opposition to such trends of thought, I feel the duty to reaffirm strongly that the intrinsic value and personal dignity of every human being do not change, no matter what the concrete circumstances of his or her life. *A man, even if seriously ill or disabled in the exercise of his highest functions, is and always will be a man*, and he will never become a "vegetable" or an "animal".

Even our brothers and sisters who find themselves in the clinical condition of a "vegetative state" retain their human dignity in all its fullness. The loving gaze of God the Father continues to fall upon them, acknowledging them as his sons and daughters, especially in need of help.

Medical doctors and health-care personnel, society and the Church have moral duties toward these persons from which they cannot exempt themselves without lessening the demands both of professional ethics and human and Christian solidarity.

The sick person in a vegetative state, awaiting recovery or a natural end, still has the right to basic health care (nutrition, hydration, cleanliness, warmth, etc.), and to the prevention of complications related to his confinement to bed. He also has the right to appropriate rehabilitative care and to be monitored for clinical signs of eventual recovery.

Death by Starvation Is a Form of Euthanasia

I should like particularly to underline how the administration of water and food, even when provided by artificial means, always represents a *natural means* of preserving life, not a *medical act.* Its use, furthermore, should be considered, in principle, *ordinary* and *proportionate*, and as such morally obligatory, insofar as and until it is seen to have attained its proper finality, which in the present case consists in providing nourishment to the patient and alleviation of his suffering.

Considerations about the 'quality of life,' often actually dictated by psychological, social and economic pressures, cannot take precedence over general principles.

The obligation to provide the "normal care due to the sick in such cases" includes, in fact, the use of nutrition and hydration. The evaluation of probabilities, founded on waning hopes for recovery when the vegetative state is prolonged beyond a year, cannot ethically justify the cessation or interruption of *minimal care* for the patient, including nutrition and hydration. Death by starvation or dehydration is, in fact, the only possible outcome as a result of their withdrawal. In this sense it ends up becoming, if done knowingly and willingly, true and proper euthanasia by omission.

In this regard, I recall what I wrote in the Encyclical *Evangelium Vitae*, making it clear that "by *euthanasia in the true and proper sense* must be understood an action or omission which by its very nature and intention brings about death, with the purpose of eliminating all pain"; such an act is always "a *serious violation of the law of God*, since it is the deliberate and morally unacceptable killing of a human person".

Besides, the moral principle is well known, according to which even the simple doubt of being in the presence of a living person already imposes the obligation of full respect and of abstaining from any act that aims at anticipating the person's death.

Protection of Human Life Is Fundamental

Considerations about the "quality of life", often actually dictated by psychological, social and economic pressures, cannot take precedence over general principles.

> *It is necessary to promote the* taking of positive actions *as a stand against pressures to withdraw hydration and nutrition as a way to put an end to the lives of these patients.*

First of all, no evaluation of costs can outweigh the value of the fundamental good which we are trying to protect, that of human life. Moreover, to admit that decisions regarding man's life can be based on the external acknowledgment of its quality, is the same as acknowledging that increasing and decreasing levels of quality of life, and therefore of human dignity, can be attributed from an external perspective to any subject, thus introducing into social relations a discriminatory and eugenic principle.

Moreover, it is not possible to rule out *a priori* that the withdrawal of nutrition and hydration, as reported by authoritative studies, is the source of considerable suffering for the sick person, even if we can see only the reactions at the level of the autonomic nervous system or of gestures. Modern clinical neurophysiology and neuro-imaging techniques, in fact, seem to point to the lasting quality in these patients of elementary forms of communication and analysis of stimuli.

However, it is not enough to reaffirm the general principle according to which the value of a man's life cannot be made subordinate to any judgment of its quality expressed by other men; it is necessary to promote the *taking of positive actions* as a stand against pressures to withdraw hydration and nutrition as a way to put an end to the lives of these patients.

Patient and Family Support Are Paramount

It is necessary, above all, *to support those families* who have had one of their loved ones struck down by this terrible clinical condition. They cannot be left alone with their heavy human, psychological and financial burden. Although the care for these patients is not, in general, particularly costly, society must allot sufficient resources for the care of this sort of frailty, by way of bringing about appropriate, concrete initiatives such as, for example, the creation of a network of awakening centres with specialized treatment and rehabilitation programmes; financial support and home assistance for families when patients are moved back home at the end of intensive rehabilitation programmes; the establishment of facilities which can accommodate those cases in which there is no family able to deal with the problem or to provide "breaks" for those families who are at risk of psychological and moral burn-out.

Proper care for these patients and their families should, moreover, include the presence and the witness of a medical doctor and an entire team, who are asked to help the family understand that they are there as allies who are in this struggle with them. The participation of volunteers represents a basic support to enable the family to break out of its isolation and to help it to realize that it is a precious and not a forsaken part of the social fabric.

In these situations, then, spiritual counselling and pastoral aid are particularly important as help for recovering the deepest meaning of an apparently desperate condition.

Distinguished ladies and gentlemen, in conclusion I exhort you, as men and women of science responsible for the dignity of the medical profession, to guard jealously the principle according to which the true task of medicine is "to cure if possible, always to care".

As a pledge and support of this, your authentic humanitarian mission to give comfort and support to your suffering brothers and sisters, I remind you of the words of Jesus: "Amen, I say to you, whatever you did for one of these least brothers of mine, you did for me" (Matthew 25:40).

6

Physician-Assisted Suicide Is Not Contrary to Christian Beliefs

John Shelby Spong

John Shelby Spong served as bishop of the Episcopal Diocese of Newark, New Jersey, for more than twenty years and is one of the leading spokespersons for liberal Christianity. He is the author of numerous books, including the best-selling Rescuing the Bible from Fundamentalism *and* Why Christianity Must Change or Die.

Conservative Christians oppose physician-assisted suicide on the grounds that the power over life and death resides with God alone. Their arguments against assisted suicide are unconvincing. In asserting that the Bible condemns suicide in any form, they ignore biblical passages that they find outdated or inconvenient. Assisted suicide violates neither the Bible nor the holiness of life. The sacredness of life is not served by forcing people to remain living in a physical body being ravaged by a terminal disease.

Editor's note: This viewpoint is taken from a speech delivered to a 2003 meeting of the Hemlock Society.

I am a practicing Christian, an ordained minister, and an elected bishop in my church. Indeed, when I retired [in 2000], I was the senior active bishop in the Episcopal Church

John Shelby Spong, Address to the National Convention of the Hemlock Society in San Diego, CA, "Death: A Friend to Be Welcomed, Not an Enemy to Be Defeated," dyingwithdignity.ca, January 10, 2003. Reproduced by permission of author.

in the United States in point of service. That represents a long career in a position of major leadership. Yet, at the same time, I deeply support physician-assisted suicide. I believe that if and when a person arrives at that point in human existence when death has become a kinder alternative than hopeless pain, and when a chronic dependency on narcotics begins to require the loss of personal dignity, then the basic human right to choose how and when to die should be guaranteed by law and respected by our communities of faith. . . .

I want to assist this audience and through this audience to assist the listening world to understand the sources of the religious negativity that hover around all of the end-of-life issues. Then I want to propose a way in which this negativity can be addressed and hopefully changed. Because I am both a Christian and a supporter of the right to determine how and when I will die, I want to demonstrate that one does not have to abandon a traditional religious commitment in order to embrace what I now regard as a compelling new freedom. . . .

The Judeo-Christian faith story opens with the assertion of life's sanctity. The creation narrative presents us with a portrait of human life as being made in the divine image. Christians have derived from this assertion that the power to live or to die is not a decision that properly resides in human beings. That power, it is typically said, belongs to God alone. Therefore, the traditional Christian concludes [that] no one can be given the liberty of ending his or her life under any circumstances.

That principle permeates Christian thinking. Yet, a look at Christian history will reveal that it has been randomly and inconsistently applied.

Christian Teachings Are Not Applied Uniformly

In the course of that history, we Christians have not left the power to die exclusively in God's hands. Rather, we have fought religious wars in which people were killed quite deliberately. God did not kill them; human beings, who called themselves Christians, did. Many of our victims were people of other religious convictions. We have justified these political acts of violence with elaborate arguments about what constitutes a "just war." I do not want to argue on this occasion either the "pacifist" position or the "just war" position. I simply want to note that in this area, Christians have not left the power of life and death in God's hands alone. We have rather abrogated this power to ourselves.

We have also employed the practice of capital punishment in the Christian nations of the Western world for almost all our history. It is only recently, and quite frankly in the more secularized nations of Western Europe, that the debate on the morality of capital punishment has led some nations to ban this practice as cruel and inhumane punishment. But the records of history show that Christian rulers in Christian nations, aided and abetted by the prevailing religious hierarchies of the Christian churches, have shown no reluctance whatsoever in claiming the right to take the power of life and death from God's hands and to place that power squarely into their own very human hands.

An Irrational Inconsistency

Christians have, over the years of their history, used their power to execute their critics again and again as part of their way of enforcing religious beliefs. A man named Giordano Bruno was burned at the stake in 1600 by the religious authorities of his day because he taught that the earth was not the center of the universe. That was, of course, a point of view contrary to the prevailing Christian synthesis.

The Inquisition used the same tactic at many different fiery stakes to execute thousands of human beings for the sin of heresy or for the "crime," as they thought of it, of being a Jew. The Crusades, officially sponsored by the Vatican, also caused the death of many Jews in Europe because Jews were the only "infidels" that the Crusaders could locate when their romantic journeys to free the holy land from such nonbelievers failed to reach its destination. . . .

If human beings who call themselves Christians have no scruples about endorsing war, killing religious enemies, or imposing the sentence of death upon those who violate either the norms of faith or the boundaries of prejudice under a set of circumstances in the past, is it still appropriate for Christians to suggest that one cannot elect death for himself or herself under a different set of circumstances in the present? It seems to me that a certain irrational inconsistency is operating here, which needs to be pointed out to any faith community that espouses such claims. . . .

Prejudice Buttressed by Biblical Quotations

Suicide, they contend, is always wrong, always a violation of the holiness of life and of the God who is the Source of Life. It is an interesting but unconvincing argument. Its weakness is best seen, however, when these same religious people play what has traditionally been their favorite and final trump card: The Bible condemns suicide in any form, they assert.

The most amazing thing about people who seek to end an argument by quoting the authority of the Bible is that most of these quoters are woefully ignorant of the content of the Bible itself. . . .

To have the Bible quoted by the religious community today to bring a final solution to all end-of-life discussions is hardly something to be feared. It is only the last gasp of religious imperialism. It needs only to be countered with informed data.

Biblical Accounts of Suicide Are Scarce

There are only three stories in the Bible about people who committed suicide. One is about King Saul, the predecessor to

King David in Jewish history. Saul had been mortally wounded in the battle of Mount Gilboa, when the Jews were fighting against the Philistines. He begged his armor bearer to strike him with his sword to end his suffering and to hasten his inevitable death. When the armor bearer refused, Saul fell on his own sword and ended his life.

The second was a man named Ahithophel, who was one of King David's advisers, who ate daily at the royal table. Ahithophel betrayed King David, who as king was called the Lord's anointed. When he [Ahithophel] was discovered, the text says, he went out and hanged himself.

The third was Judas Iscariot, whose story was clearly shaped by the account of Ahithophel. He also ate at the Lord's table. He also was said to have betrayed one known as the Lord's anointed. When Judas was discovered, he, like Ahithophel, went out and hanged himself.

The Biblical writers assumed that for Ahithophel and Judas Iscariot, suicide was an appropriate punishment for their crimes. They are surprisingly ambivalent about King Saul.

While the Bible does appear to be generally negative about suicide, it does not seem to condemn those who take somebody else's life. That appears to be true even with the commandment "Thou shalt not kill" as part of its legal code.

New Duties for a New Age

If you read the Bible carefully, you will discover that this book prescribes the death penalty for such crimes as worshiping false gods; for being disobedient; for talking back to or cursing your parents; for being a medium, a wizard, or a witch; for committing adultery; and even for having a sexual affair with your mother-in-law. Since few people ever quote this verse about one's mother-in-law, probably because they cannot imagine anyone being guilty of such an act, I share with you that the text is found in Leviticus 20:14.

If life is too sacred for one to seek release from it under any circumstances, does it not also become too sacred to have it taken away by another?

We have watched human life actually evolve to where it must accept God-like responsibilities. The time has come to celebrate that, not to hide from it.

I, as a Christian, believe that life is sacred, that it is the ultimate gift of God. Because I hold this belief, I am committed to living every moment that I am given as deeply, richly and fully as I can. But both the times in which you and I live and the shape of our consciousness in many areas of life have changed dramatically through the ages. Human knowledge has expanded enormously, which means that "new occasions teach new duties," as the poet James Russell Lowell once observed. I today can no longer just quote the wisdom of antiquity as a passive observer of life. It is not enough just to be a committed Christian; I must also take seriously what it means to be a citizen of the 21st century.

I am the beneficiary of a vast revolution in scientific and medical thinking. I possess a reservoir of data that was not available to the people who authored the Bible. This is the gift of the modern world to me. I have watched life expectancy expand remarkably. I live in a world of quadruple heart bypasses, chemo and radiation therapy, laproscopic surgical procedures and organ transplants, PSA tests and pap smears, miracle drugs and incredible life-support systems. My grandfather died of pneumonia. It was before the development of penicillin. I have had two diseases which I do not believe my grandparents would have survived.

Human Achievements Bestow God-like Powers

I live in a privileged part of the world and in a privileged generation. I rejoice in all of these human achievements. But let there be no mistake about what is happening. These stirring achievements represent human beings taking on the power we once ascribed only to God. We have, by our own knowledge and expertise, put our hands on the decisions about life and death. We cannot now refuse to engage these decisions at the end of our own lives. We have pushed back the boundaries of death inexorably. We have enabled this generation to live in a way that previous generations could never have imagined. We have watched human life actually evolve to where it must accept God-like responsibilities. The time has come to celebrate that, not to hide from it in the language of piety.

Do we human beings, including those of us who claim to be Christian, not have the right to say, 'That is not the way I choose to die?' I believe we do!

What I see the religious community doing today is to tremble in the face of our own human audacity and to seek to hide from the responsibility inherent in our own human achievements, none of which we would be willing to surrender. Why else would we hesitate before this final boundary called death? Why would we resist so vigorously the reality that now we must take a hand in our death decision? When medical science expands the boundary and the quality of life, Christians do not complain. We, rather, rejoice because we believe it affirms our conviction that life is holy.

It is one thing, however, to expand life and it is quite another to postpone death. When medical science shifts from expanding the length and quality of life and begins simply to postpone the reality of death, why are we not capable of saying that the sacredness of life is no longer being served?

Death Is Not the Enemy

What happens to both our courage and our faith? Is a breathing cadaver, with no hope of restoration, an example of the sacredness of life? I do not think so! Do we human beings, including those of us who claim to be Christian, not have the right to say, "That is not the way I choose to die?" I believe we do!

I honor the God of life whom I serve by living fully. I do not honor this God by clinging to a life that has become an empty shell.

Is death really the enemy, as St. Paul once stated? On that definition, so much Christian thinking has been based. Well, let it be said by a bishop of the church: *St. Paul was wrong*! He was wrong here and in several other places. I often wonder how it was that the words of this man ever came to be called "The Word of God." When Paul said, "I hope those who bother you will mutilate themselves," was that the word of God? Paul was a child of his era responding to his presuppositions and living with his prejudices. They are not mine. I prefer to think of death not as an enemy but as a friend, even a brother, as St. Francis of Assisi once suggested. The time has therefore come, I believe, for Christians to embrace death not as an enemy to be defeated, but as an aspect of life's holiness to be embraced. Death is life's shadow. It walks with us through the entire course of our days. We embrace death as a friend because we honor life. I honor the God of life whom I serve by living fully. I do not honor this God by clinging to a life that has become an empty shell.

I do not honor life when I fail to see that death and finitude are what gives life its precious quality. Death is not punishment for sin, as Paul also once suggested and as classical Christianity has long maintained. Death is an aspect of life, a vital aspect that gives life its deepest flavor, its defining sensitivity.

Death Is an Inescapable Reality

Someone once observed that "death rings the bell on all procrastination." It is because life is finite, not infinite, that we do not postpone the quest for meaning indefinitely. It is because of the presence of death with us on our life's journey that we do not fail to take the opportunity to say "I love you," to invest ourselves in primary relationships, to do what needs to be done to build a better world now. Death says you do not have forever to make a difference. Death is what gives conscious life its uniqueness. Remove death from life and life becomes enduring boredom, an endless game of shuffleboard. We make life precious by embracing the reality of death, not by repressing it or denying it. Our present burial customs of making up the faces of the deceased so that they look natural and using artificial grass to cover the dirt of the grave rise out of the fear of our mortality, not out of our affirmation about the wonder and beauty of life.

My deepest desire is always to choose death with dignity over a life that has become either hopelessly painful and dysfunctional or empty and devoid of all meaning.

I, for one, want to live my life by wringing every ounce of joy out of every moment that I am given. I want to expand my life to its fullest extent. That is the way that the sacredness of life is affirmed. I want to drink deeply of life's sweetness. I want to scale life's heights and plumb its depths. I want to do all I can do to affirm life and, yes, to postpone death at least until life's quality has been so compromised that it is no longer life as I believe God created it. Then I want to embrace death as my friend, my companion who has walked with me from the first moment I was born.

Dying with Dignity

I want to live my days surrounded by those I love, able to see my wife's smiling face, and to experience the joy and vitality of my children and grandchildren. But when those realities begin to fade away, then I want to leave this world, and those I love, with a positive vision. I want them to see in me one who lived and loved deeply and well, until living and loving deeply and well was no longer possible. I want them to remember me as a person who was vital to the end, as one who was in possession of all that makes me who I am, and as one who died well. My deepest desire is always to choose death with dignity over a life that has become either hopelessly painful and dysfunctional or empty and devoid of all meaning.

That is the only way I know that would allow me to honor the God in whose image I believe I was created. That is the way I want to acknowledge the relationship I have had with God, which has grown from a dependent and immature one into the maturity of recognizing that to be human is to share with God in the ultimate life and death decisions. That is how I hope and expect to celebrate both life's holiness and life's Creator. That does not seem to me to be too much to ask of either my faith or my government.

Assisted Suicide Should Be Lawful

I think this choice should be legal. I will work, therefore, through the political processes to seek to create a world where advance directives are obeyed and where physicians will assist those, who choose to do so, with the ability to die at the appropriate time. I also think the choice to do this should be acclaimed as both moral and ethical, a human right if you will, and I will work through the ecclesiastical processes of my church and all the forces of organized religion to change consciousness, to embrace new realities, and to enable Christians and other people of faith to say that we are compelled in this direction because we believe that God is real and life is holy. The God whom I experience as the Source of Life can surely not be served by those in whom death is simply postponed after real life has departed.

I close with a text, because people seem to believe that a clergyman must have a text for every speech that he or she delivers. In the 10th Chapter of John's Gospel, these words are attributed to that Jesus of Nazareth who stands at the center of my faith tradition. Articulating his purpose, He says: "I have come that you might have life and that you might have it abundantly." It is that abundant life which is the ultimate gift of God. I walk into the Source of that abundant life in the way I live. I also want to walk into the Source of that abundant life in the way I die.

I see no contradiction between the faith I cherish and principles for which the Hemlock Society stands. I embrace your conclusions with the hope that you will listen to, heed, and welcome the pathway of faith that I have traveled that enables me to stand at your side today and to claim you as my ally in the struggle to discover the ultimate meaning of life itself. I am a Christian whose faith has led him to champion the legal, moral, and ethical right that I believe every individual should be given—to die with dignity and to have the freedom to choose when and how that dignified death might be accomplished.

7

Assisted Suicide Is Moral

Andrew C. Markus

Andrew Markus is an emeritus fellow at Green College, Oxford University, in Great Britian.

A doctor's involvement in assisting a suicide does not conflict, in principle, with the basic aims of medicine. Helping the sick may involve a wide spectrum of activity, and assisted suicide may be one venue through which such help can be rendered. Choosing when and how a person will exit this life is a very personal decision. From this perspective, helping terminally ill patients to end their lives for the purpose of alleviating intense physical or mental suffering is both rational and compassionate.

I write as a family doctor, and even though retired, I still think like one and like to base my musings on a case history:

A highly placed diplomat with splendid prospects was married to, and deeply in love with, a very beautiful woman. He was a man of humble origins and could never quite understand how such a gorgeous and good woman could have agreed to marry him—his self-esteem was surprisingly limited considering the position he held.

One of his colleagues was jealous of him and fed this low self-esteem by suggesting that his wife might be having an affair. Gradually distrust festered and eventually, after being given some false evidence of infidelity, the diplomat strangled

Andrew C. Markus, "Life or Death, Mad or Sane—Who Decides?" *Perspectives in Biology and Medicine*, vol. 45, Spring 2002, pp. 264–272.

his wife. She screamed as he was killing her and instantly the room was filled with people who had heard her.

They were appalled and quickly made him realize that he had suspected her without justification.

Using a knife he had on his person he committed suicide.

Should the crowd standing around Othello, for he it was [in Shakespeare's play], have tried to stop him? Or was he entitled to make a decision that life would no longer be worth living without his wife, disgraced, and perhaps in prison for the rest of his life? And if a doctor, and in particular a psychiatrist, had been present, would he or she, as part of their professional duty, have been under obligation to stop him on the grounds that anyone contemplating suicide is ipso facto incompetent to make an autonomous decision?

The Suicide Conundrum

It is part of the human condition to believe that living is better than not living, otherwise life makes no sense and gives us no purpose—unless, of course, we believe that this life is only a preparation for another.

If we accept that life is in general preferable to death, how does suicide fit in? In the United Kingdom, suicide has been legal since the 1960s, on the assumption that a fully competent individual can make an autonomous decision that no life is preferable to life.

To give drugs to assist pain relief which have the secondary effect of hastening death is legal and generally considered acceptable.

Yet many people would argue that no one in their "right mind" would commit suicide—in other words, that persons planning suicide should be restrained from carrying out their plans, to have their autonomy overruled, in order to stop them. Jonathan Glover has written that one good reason for stopping someone from committing suicide is that it gives the person a second chance, but it is unlikely that Othello would have changed his mind, and many would think he did the right thing.

I have thought about this conundrum over the years, partly in connection with my clinical role as a doctor and partly from the point of view of my contact with psychiatry. My interest was particularly aroused by my colleague and friend, Keith Hawton, now one of the professors of psychiatry in Oxford, who spoke about his work on suicide in the United Kingdom perhaps 15 years ago—he continues to research in this area. Many learned books and papers have been written around this subject. My article, by a non-specialist, is aimed at triggering discussion rather than examining these issues in detail.

Is a Standard Ethical Approach Possible?

So I would like you to consider a number of diffuse but conflicting statements. Though suicide is legal, to assist someone to commit suicide is not. To give drugs to assist pain relief which have the secondary effect of hastening death is legal and generally considered acceptable (a demonstration of the concept of double effect, which will be considered later). We as doctors are exhorted by the U.K. government to reduce the incidence of suicide, and yet we need to respect the autonomous decisions of our competent patients. But a patient who commits suicide in hospital or prison is considered to have done so as a result of failure by staff to prevent it. In addition, we know that many suicides occur in people who are suffering from a relapsing condition such as depression, and that though suicide is an act involving an individual only, it almost invariably causes major trauma to relatives and friends.

I would like to use these statements as a way into considering suicide and physician-assisted suicide and just touching on euthanasia, from the point of view of both general medicine and psychiatry, and as a means for ascertaining how a standard ethical approach may or may not help.

Is there a duty by the medical profession to prevent suicide in whatever form, or is this part of the 'nanny state' interfering in the autonomous wishes of individuals?

Attitudes Against Assisted Suicide Have Softened

The attitude to physician-assisted suicide and voluntary euthanasia has become more liberal latterly, especially in Holland but also in the United Kingdom. In August 2000, a case was reported in the *British Medical Journal* in which the High Court in London decided that a man aged 19, who was suffering from motor neuron disease, had the right to die when he could no longer blink with his left eye—his only means of communication. At the same time doctors and especially psychiatrists are charged by the government with a reduction in suicide rates, presumably on the assumption that anyone, or maybe the majority, contemplating suicide must be suffering from a psychiatric illness. Some are, mainly from depression, but many are not.

Is there a duty by the medical profession to prevent suicide in whatever form, or is this part of the "nanny state" interfering in the autonomous wishes of individuals?

Although suicide itself was legalized in the United Kingdom in 1961, a House of Lords commission in 1994 advised against any loosening of laws on euthanasia for fear of developing a "slippery slope" situation. In the interval, surveys have shown that there has been a softening of public opinion on the admissibility of both active euthanasia and "passive"—that is, the withholding of treatment for persons such as those suffering from a persistent vegetative state.

This public softening of attitudes that has taken place in the United Kingdom and more so in Holland has happened mainly in the context of those suffering from physical illnesses, and it depends on persons being either competent to make such decisions themselves or being so persistently unconscious as to require decisions to be made by others. The concept of competence, which requires the ability to comprehend and retain information and the ability to weigh up such information in order to come to a choice is particularly difficult to apply to patients with mental illness.

I would like now to consider three fundamental issues that emerge from what I have said already.

Is There Value in Suffering?

In general, humans exhibit a "will to live"—we are programmed this way. This implies that life, and the continuation of it, has value, and that the old-fashioned U.K. Coroner's verdict of "suicide whilst the balance of mind was disturbed" is an appropriate summing up of the situation: one would be mad to end life. Yet we seem to accept that those who choose to neglect themselves, for instance by not eating enough or living rough, are placing a lower value on life than on other priorities, as are those who indulge in dangerous sports or who consider that, without taking risks, "life would not be worth living." Similarly, a competent patient on a life-support machine is entitled to choose to ask for the machine to be switched off, so as to be "allowed to die"—and this is not classed as suicide. An element of free choice has entered.

The basic question then is whether the despair that leads to considering life not worth living is justified in the context of a normal perception of the world.

The Judeo-Christian religious viewpoint is that life is God-given and that though we are also given free will, it is always wrong to (willfully) terminate our own life. Out of this conundrum has appeared the concept of the value of suffering—a concept I find myself totally unable to subscribe to. Paradoxically, too, the life of others may be taken in self-defense or during war.

Life Must Have Meaning

If such a religious viewpoint is excluded, and the exercise of choice is within the frame, we have to think in terms of life having meaning, or value, to go on being worthwhile. This meaning may take the form of doing things we find give satisfaction—such as being a doctor or writing fiction or being involved in making the streets clean—or of being able to conduct relationships with others. All of these involve gaining the respect of people we are in contact with, which helps us to have respect for ourselves—to have value.

Even if such meanings are not present, there may be some hope that they will be in the future. The abandonment of hope leads to despair, which may then lead to the contemplation of suicide. But while terminal illness with the prospect of suffering may seem a reasonable justification, being jilted in a relationship at the age of 17 may not. The basic question then is whether the despair that leads to considering life not worth living is justified in the context of a normal perception of the world, or whether it arises because of some temporary distortion of perception, such as happens with mood swings or in mental illness. And who makes the judgement as to justification? In other words, who decides in the border area between rational thinking and mental illness?

Suicide and the Mentally Ill

The comment that "They must be mad to do it" suggests that anyone contemplating suicide must be suffering from a mental illness, and that it is for doctors, especially psychiatrists, to cure such illness. But are all those suffering from a mental illness, by definition, unable to make a competent decision? How much misery and despair should persons suffer before it is accepted that it is reasonable for them to make a decision to terminate their lives? As already mentioned, when considering physical illness, it would generally be accepted that persons suffering from a painful and incurable illness should be listened to and allowed to die if they wish—with passive if not active assistance from the doctor in charge. In a situation where someone is suffering from persistent lack of enjoyment of life, with no possible relief in sight, but with no clinical mental illness on board, should not the same consideration operate? Indeed, should not someone suffering from a recurrent mental illness that shows no sign of being controllable by medication, and that perhaps causes chaos to those around, be granted the "accolade" of "incurable illness" to justify the wish to die—of course if the wish is expressed during a normal period? As so often, [author] Saul Bellow has summed up the dilemma for the individual: "Maybe an unexamined life is not worth living. But a man's examined life can make him wish he was dead."

My own feeling is that, on the whole, autonomy should be allowed to trump.

And even if some form of treatment is available, is it reasonable to force people to submit to it, even to take away their autonomy by forcefully hospitalizing them, if they do not wish to have treatment?

A much-quoted case which raised this issue, and many others with which I won't deal, occurred in Holland in the early 1990s. Mrs. Bosscher was about 50 years old and had been unhappily married for some 30 years. She lived for her two sons, and when one committed suicide and a few years later the other died of cancer, she felt that all purpose in her life had vanished and she made a suicide attempt, which failed.

She then approached a Dr. Chabot for assistance—in fact for euthanasia, though I don't want to deal with that aspect at the moment. What is relevant to my present point is that after lengthy psychiatric assessment, only a "complex adjustment reaction" and no evidence of clinical depression or other psychiatric illness was demonstrated. She refused any attempt at psychological treatment. There was therefore no evidence that she was incompetent to make a decision that her life should be terminated. That Dr. Chabot administered a fatal injection is not the issue here. The issue is that she was suffering from continuing mental distress, from despair, and yet by normal assessment she was competent to make a decision that she wanted to end her life.

My own feeling is that, on the whole, autonomy should be allowed to trump.

As Death Approaches: The Doctor's Role

Should doctors ever be involved in causing the death of patients, by commission or omission? And is the concept of "double effect" —the principle that determines when an action that has both good and bad results is morally permissible—a valid one? You will notice that I add the qualifying phrase "by commission or omission," because I would contend that there is really no fundamental difference between acts of commission and those of omission, if the same end result is achieved by two routes. A doctor may withhold antibiotics in a patient with terminal cancer, knowing that this will result in the patient's earlier demise, and because this is an act of omission it is considered permissible, even though the doctor knows full well that the patient's death is being hastened. Concepts in relation to the turning off of a life-support machine have evolved over the years. The well-publicised case of Tony Bland illustrates this. He was a young man who was injured in the Hillsborough football stadium disaster in 1989 and descended into a persistent vegetative state, thus making him incompetent to make a decision. It took a court ruling some years later to allow feeding to be stopped. This is in contrast to the case of the 19-year-old with motor neuron disease already mentioned—the difference, of course, being that the latter was competent to make a decision, thus allowing the doctors to actively switch off the machine.

In this area the law in Britain is easing, as are public attitudes, but to me the distinction between a doctor hastening a patient's death by active or passive means is not clear.

The Double-Effect Doctrine Is Obsolete

I would also like to deal with what I now consider to be the outdated concept of "double effect." The doctrine of double effect implies that one is allowed to take an action that may result in death if procuring death is not the primary intention of that action, but it is not allowable to take the same action with the primary purpose of causing death. For instance, one can prescribe a large dose of morphine to control a physically ill patient's pain, even though this may shorten the patient's life, but one cannot prescribe the same dose with the primary intention of killing the patient. [Moral philosopher] Baroness [Mary] Warnock maintains that this is very much an argument for "getting off the hook." Catholic theology maintains that it is never permissible to perform an immoral act in order to permit something good to happen, and that a clear distinction can be drawn between what is intended and what is a secondary—but nevertheless anticipated—result of an action.

A widely reported case has recently arisen in the United Kingdom in which a court was involved over the separation of Siamese twins. It was known that if they were separated, one would live and the other die. The court eventually gave permission and this is what happened. Although the death of the second twin was not the primary intent of the intervention, it was anticipated and directly caused by the surgeon's action. Therefore, to my mind, it cannot be excused on the grounds of double effect. If an excuse is required, it must be on the basis of weighing up of the consequences of the intervention and deciding that causing this death was acceptable.

To return, then, to whether it is ever permissible for a doctor to kill a patient, we have just seen one example of where it probably is. Perhaps the best way forward is to consider what doctors should be doing for their patients. *Bartlett's Medical Quotations* includes a folk saying in French which translated reads, "Cure sometimes, help often, comfort always." Hippocrates encapsulated it in "Helping the sick."

There Is No Universal Moral Order

Those who are opposed to the involvement of any doctor in the purposeful termination of life argue that to do so would violate the moral integrity of medicine and that doctors should never be involved in intentional killing. In our society this is partly the aftermath of the horrific involvement of doctors in the eugenic and medical experimentation policies of Nazi Germany. As we have already seen, this argument does not wholly reflect what does happen at the moment. Though some argue that a universal moral order exists that decrees certain ways of behaving, others, myself among them, would strongly argue that what is expected of a physician in society is a social construct, sanctioned by the laws of that society and open to rational debate. I have already mentioned the shifting situation in Holland and to a certain extent in the United Kingdom. In Japan, neither of the major religions, Shintoism and Buddhism, prohibit suicide, and many literary works extol it as a way to atone for misdeeds. Interestingly, there are still strict laws in place against euthanasia and physician-assisted suicide, though individual judgements have breached these rules. In the United States, Oregon passed a law permitting physician-assisted suicide in 1997. Between November of that year and July 1998, there were eight doctor-assisted suicides there, though the federal government under President [Bill]

Clinton expressed reservations. It is likely that the present [George W. Bush] administration's policies will be more negative.

In principle, medical involvement in suicide, or for that matter euthanasia, does not conflict with the basic aims of medicine of helping the sick.

Acting in the Patients' Best Interests

The purpose of benefiting the sick may involve a wide spectrum of activity, and some would consider that it may involve stopping the suffering of a patient by terminating life, and that this suffering may cover both physical and psychological situations. I have heard it argued that patients would lose faith in doctors if they knew that doctors may sometimes terminate life, and yet on many occasions I have had patients pleading with me to do just that, to put an end to their psychological or physical suffering.

It could be that in a large area of patient care, doctors are not actually doing what patients themselves feel would be in their best interests. I know that in my own case this has to do with my own abhorrence of the possibility that I am purposefully killing someone. However, my rational self suggests that in principle, medical involvement in suicide, or for that matter euthanasia, does not conflict with the basic aims of medicine of helping the sick, though I am well aware of the strength of the "slippery slope" argument. It may even be that taking seriously the wishes of patients who suffer from incurable physical illness, or even despair, may actually enhance trust in the doctor-patient relationship. For myself—and this is my problem—I just wouldn't be able to be the person giving the lethal medicine. I agree with [Dr. Bernard] Baumrin in his contribution to Battin, Rhodes, and Silvers [1998 book *Physician-Assisted Suicide*], that if euthanasia were to be legalized, it should be administered by someone other than a doctor.

I don't know what I would have done if I had been present at the bedroom scene where Desdemona lay dead and Othello was stabbing himself. I guess, though, that I would not have tried to intervene. Should I have realized that I was party to causing death by omission and have felt guilty?

8

Assisted Suicide Is Not the Solution to Pain and Suffering

Richard Radtke

Richard Radtke is the president and chief executive officer of the Sea of Dreams Foundation, a nonprofit organization dedicated to providing disabled individuals with educational opportunites. A retired professor of biological oceanography, Radtke holds continuing graduate faculty status at the University of Hawaii.

Proponents of assisted suicide claim that such an option is necessary in order to alleviate the pain and suffering of dying patients; however, assisted suicide is not the answer for people facing life-threatening illnesses and disabilities. Instead, the medical community must offer better pain management, better palliative care, and access to hospice. In addition, society needs to encourage and assist disabled people to develop their potential and achieve a satisfactory quality of life. If society provides these supports, people facing death and the loss of bodily functions will be able to live with hope and dignity and will not seek to end their lives through assisted suicide.

The discussion about physician-assisted suicide often centers on the issues of unbearable pain and dignity. Issues are often wrought with attitude bias, clouded perceptions, and fear. Most individuals when asked whether they or others should suffer unbearable pain and an undignified demise would state a resounding "no." No one wants anyone to

Richard Radtke, "A Case Against Physician-Assisted Suicide," *Journal of Disability Policy Studies*, vol. 16, Summer 2005, pp. 58–61. Copyright 2005 PRO–ED, Inc. Reprinted with permission.

suffer, and everyone deserves dignity. However, let us not allow the arguments on assisted suicide to cloud the major issues of better pain management, palliative care and hospice, and an increased quality of life, which would make this issue a moot point. We need to work toward better life, not toward ways to end it.

Lest you think my convictions are based on a foundation of naiveté and self delusion, I will use myself and the experiences of my life as a case study.

My condition is incurable. My original prognosis was that I would be dead [by the summer of 2000] from the rapid progression of my disease. I have lost many bodily functions. I cannot move from the neck down. For the entire first 2 years of my disability, I have to admit, I was very depressed. I had to ask people for help where I never had to ask for help before. During that darkest period, I thought about suicide. If procedures were available to help me end my life, I might well be dead now. I think still physician-assisted suicide is wrong.

People Adjust to Disability

People with illness and disability are statistically more likely to have feelings of suicide, especially in the early period after the onset of a significant disability because of psychosocial issues, such as feeling like a burden on family and fears about future loss of function associated with increases in disability. However, research overwhelmingly shows that after an adjustment period, people with disabilities rate their own quality of life as high or higher than [does] the general public. People with disabilities are very familiar with these issues, but let me continue with my case study.

I was diagnosed with multiple sclerosis (MS) around 1980. I was married, had already finished my doctoral degree in fisheries oceanography, and had started a research position at the University of Hawaii. My MS is chronic progressive, so it progressed very quickly. In about 2 years I was in a wheelchair, and about 3 years later, I was a quadriplegic. Then, 3 years after that, my wife divorced me.

It is difficult when we encounter disability to see clearly what is possible and where life is going to take us.

I'm 6'4″ tall and had been very active as a young man. I grew up on a farm and played sports all the way through high school and college. My transition to disability was very abrupt, and I experienced a lot of the problems that people talk about when they consider physician-assisted suicide. They talk about their personal concerns—losing their autonomy, losing their control over bodily functions. There is a tremendous amount of fear when you first confront these changes. If you go from playing football to being a quadriplegic within a 5-year period, it changes your life. When you go from moving furniture to having someone help you wipe your butt that is a transition! I didn't want to do it at first. Actually, I didn't want to do it at all. If someone were to say, "We're going to take you from being a strong healthy person to someone who is reliant on others," nobody is going to say they want to do that.

Visualizing the Future Can Be Hard

After my wife left, I had no conception of what my life would be like now. At that point, I figured it was over. I was basically alone. I had assistance to go to bed and accomplish other daily tasks, but I felt everything that mattered was just crumbling all around me. Really, I was looking for support to live, not die, but I didn't know what I needed or how to accomplish what I wanted to do. I had to learn a lot. I could not imagine that 12 years later, I'd have a second wife, a daughter, and everything that fills my world now. It is difficult when we encounter disability to see clearly what is possible and where life is going to take us.

When I finally came through those years, I realized I had different parts to my life. I look at my past before MS, and I look at my present. I realize that it is similar to what most people experience as they face aging. As we get older, we experience losses. We look to a lot of people who are much older than us for their advice and their example to lead us through. When you go through a disability, the losses may seem accelerated and overwhelming. But losses come with life.

People who have disabilities must be able to reach out and feel that they are part of the world.

From personal experience, when I was diagnosed with MS, which in my case came on very rapidly, the feelings of despair and the fear of being a burden were tremendous. It took me 2 years to travel through this "phase" in life. That was over 20 years ago, and I came through this phase "stronger" than ever. Today, I have an extremely full and happy life. Life is good. The happiness I've felt and given far exceeds any discomfort I've experienced. Fear and perception can do a great disservice to everyone's lives and need to be alleviated.

Providing a Safety Net of Support

Going through any type of disability takes mental, emotional, and social support: There should be counseling to support self-esteem, there should be employment support and transportation support, looking at what options may be possible. People who have disabilities must be able to reach out and feel that they are part of the world. When you are closed in, your whole world becomes smaller and smaller. You feel that there are few options left.

Let us look at autonomy. I have to ask people for help for everything from putting on my headset for my computer to helping me eat to the one people have the most fear about—going to the bathroom. That is part of my life; and, after a while, it's become just life. We all do things that, if you stopped and pondered them, you might say, "Maybe I don't want to do these things, but I can't stop them."

With the legalization of assisted suicide, we will lose a lot of people who can make a difference.

You can't stop going to the bathroom, you can't stop eating. When I was depressed, I considered cutting my losses by "checking out." I did not see how I could maintain my sense of autonomy if I was so reliant on help.

Now, let's look at what I'm doing today. I spent 20 years as a research professor at the University of Hawaii. I've published more than 70 papers. I'm considered an expert in my field. I retired from the university in July [2005]. I'm now the president and CEO of the Sea of Dreams Foundation, which is a full-time organization set up to assist people with disabilities. We have a camp for youth with disabilities to support activities that build their self-esteem. All those things could have been lost 20 years ago if I had had someone to help me commit suicide.

The Disabled Can Contribute to Society

I have gone through a lot of soul searching. Immediately after becoming paralyzed, I believed I was of little use to people. In time, I discovered that I can make a valuable contribution, but in different ways. I serve on about six boards of directors. I'm able to help people, and I need people to help me. Help comes in different forms. The way that I contribute is different—very different—but I learned that it is possible to make a difference in this world, no matter what situation you are put into. With the legalization of assisted suicide, we will lose a lot of people who can make a difference. We cannot even dream of what those losses might be right now; we would never know.

But the fear of disability is real. Every time I travel I see it on people's faces, from getting on a plane to eating at a restaurant. People often treat you as they think they would be treated if they had a disability. The disability is not the frightening part; attitudes are.

Let us spend our time, money, and effort working on pain management rather than on ways to hasten death.

Some people may challenge my position against assisted suicide, pointing out that I had advanced education, resources, or personal strengths that others may not have to face a life with a disability. My answer is that we must find ways to give these supports to others, as it may make a life-and-death difference. You don't need a PhD to get through severe losses in your life. I have seen people go through terrible times in the small community where I grew up in Indiana. There is a resiliency in that community that gets them through. I don't know whether I consider myself a particularly strong person. I do consider myself focused, but being focused or having inner strength are qualities that people can acquire.

Hastening Death Is Not the Answer

I have also heard the argument that assisted suicide must be available for individuals with unmanageable pain. I suffer from trigeminal neuralgia, an inflammation of one of the nerves in my face. This goes along with my MS and has been described as the worst pain known to man. The pain does not even respond to morphine, so I take a whole series of medications. There are more options available through medicine today than ever before to make life more comfortable. Let us spend our time, money, and effort working on pain management rather than on ways to hasten death.

We all have a private right to suicide. I am paralyzed from the neck down, but I could kill myself if I were determined to die. Assisted suicide brings another person into the act. When someone who is desperate brings another person into the picture, I think they may be asking for help. It is not appropriate for medical science, which is set up to save and support lives, to create suddenly a function for ending lives. It is not appropriate to bring another person into a suicide.

At the time that I was diagnosed, the doctors were not very supportive. One of the doctors said, "You have multiple sclerosis," and I said, "OK, what do we do about that?" He said, "There's not much you can do right now, and if something happens it'll probably show up in the newspapers before I know about it." I never saw that doctor again. I went to a neurologist who gave me a book about [the] medical aspects of disability. It made my fears worse. I needed information about having a full life with a disability. So, I read everything I could find. I read everything on my disease so I could understand it. I read about different treatments. I read about knowing myself, all the self-help books. I tried to get as much knowledge as I could, so I could figure out what was going on with me and my inner thoughts.

Our efforts should focus on making our communities more responsive to those who need help to live, rather than figuring out these policies to help people die.

Overcoming Fear Is Our Biggest Challenge

You can imagine the thrashing my self-esteem took when I was first faced with extreme disability. At that time I found out that a lot of my self-esteem was based on my physical abilities. Having seen books that told of what appeared to me to be the horrors of being a quadriplegic—having to depend on someone else, no longer having the freedom to come and go, and basically being cut off from the so-called normal world—shook my very being.

Everyone encountering a disability should have resources addressing their spiritual life, emotional life, financial life, and medical life to help with the problems and fears that they experience. There is a big fear of being a burden on family finances, society, the world. Feeling like a burden on your family and friends is devastating. Nobody wants to be a burden. There is so much fear in our society of having a disability and needing help. Let us deal with the fear rather than resorting to assisted suicide. We can work on programs that offer respite for caregivers. Our efforts should focus on making our communities more responsive to those who need help to live, rather than figuring out these policies to help people die.

It may look different from the American dream, but I am happy with my life. When my first wife left, it seemed like the end of everything. Now I am married to a woman who has known me only as a wheelchair user and who accepts and loves me as I am. We have a 9-year-old child. I have a service dog, a beautiful animal. We live well because of all the things that I do. The fact that I work often surprises people. They wonder what the hell a paralyzed man can do other than watch TV. I do a tremendous amount of computer work. I can use the phone with a whistle switch, and as I sit by my computer now, my wife is at the market and my daughter is in the yard playing, in my care.

Taking Charge When Things Get Tough

Other points to consider are individual free choice (it is easy to have coercion under duress), the length of life (it is difficult for anyone to predict how long someone will live; medical science is an inaccurate art that changes daily), quality of life (whose scale do we use?), and the prospect for harsher application of assisted suicide (once one group is subjected, it is easier to open it to other groups). Feelings of duress because of financial and care-taking concerns repress "free choice" and cloud our perceptions of quality of life. In the absence of any real choice and in the face of duress, death by assisted suicide becomes not an act of personal autonomy but an act of desperation. Furthermore, once we accept suicide as "therapy" we become more accepting of its "applications" to other groups. This would be an insidious breach of our approach to living and dying.

I remember a turning point for me very distinctly. One night after my divorce, I was sitting there, talking to myself, saying, "Well, I only have two choices here. I'm either living the life that I want to live or I'm not living at all. If I'm going to live the life that I want to live, then I'm going to take charge of things and see what I can do to make my desires come true." That is what I chose to do. When things got tough, I remember crying a lot, but I also remember a lot of times of being happy. I had a friend of mine who told me once, "If you feel pain, you can sure as hell feel pleasure." He was right.

9

Activists Must Fight for the Right to Assisted Suicide

Derek Humphry

Formerly a London Sunday Times *reporter, Derek Humphry founded the Hemlock Society USA in 1980 and the Euthanasia Research and Guidance Organization in 1993. He is the author of six books on euthanasia. Some of his best-known works include* Jean's Way, The Right to Die, Final Exit, *and* Dying with Dignity.

The right-to-die movement has come a long way since the 1930s, but much remains to be done to ensure that the terminally and hopelessly ill can expedite their passing by availing themselves of assisted suicide or euthanasia. More doctors and nurses must become active in the cause. Their presence would further efforts toward law reform and legalization. In addition, activists must strive to change the public's perception of assisted death, soften religious opposition to this practice, and recruit a few doctors to defy existing laws and create further opportunities for successful litigation.

When we look at what the right-to-die movement has achieved, against what it has wished to do, an honest person would agree that there is still a long, long way to go.

The first signs of organized activity on this issue came in the late 1930s in Britain, but nothing really happened until the 1970s when the public—the non-medical world—woke up

Derek Humphry, Address to the 15th World Conference of the Euthanasia Research and Guidance Organization in Tokyo, "The Future of the Right-to-Die Movement," www.assistedsuicide.org, September 22, 2004. Reproduced by permission of the author.

with a shock to the fact that we often die differently nowadays compared to our ancestors.

This revelation—first made famous and characterized by the 'Karen Ann Quinlan pull-the-plug case in America'—brought a rush of legislation introducing the so-called "Living Wills"—better known nowadays as Advance Directives, permitting the disconnection—or declining the use of—pointless life support equipment.

Today Advance Directives are available pretty well everywhere. That fight has largely been won, although the problem remains in getting people to appreciate their significance and sign them early enough before terminal ill health appears. Living Wills continually need to be improved to keep pace with medical advances and updated by the signators, even young people.

Where we have even further—much further—to go is related to active voluntary euthanasia and assisted suicide for the terminally ill adult, and the hopelessly ill person. So far only the Netherlands and Belgium legally allow the first and second procedures, whilst Switzerland and Oregon allow assisted suicide. All the procedures mentioned here have strong rules and guidelines to prevent abuse.

The Fight for Assisted Suicide Continues

Actually helping people who desire a hastened death so as to avoid further suffering has a long fight ahead of it. There is stiff opposition. The underlying taboo in social life and the opposition of religious leaders in the rest of the Western world is holding back progress despite the knowledge that at a minimum—judging by electoral votes and opinion polls—fifty percent of the general public wishes to see reform to give them an eventual certain death with dignity. Other opinion testings shows 70 to 80 percent support for law reform.

The main problem is: how do we convert the converted into actual voters? The experience in America, probably the only place where actual citizens have on six occasions been asked to ballot for a right-to-die law, there are early indications that law reform will pass. Then, as the voters get to place their YEA or NAY on the ballot paper, many appear to have doubts. Except for the successful polls in Oregon in 1994 and 1996, the ballot initiatives have all failed.

Why is that? Many excuses have been offered, but my conclusion is that because we are not yet carrying a majority of the medical and nursing professions in support of us, the public—understandably—panics. Who amongst us is brave enough to defy our personal medical advisors?

Because we are not yet carrying a majority of the medical and nursing professions in support of us, the public—understandably—panics.

Of course, not all doctors and nurses will ever support us. They are entitled to have religious and ethical differences. Yet only when we have a majority of them on our side—and saying so publicly—can we be assured that future law reform will succeed.

Winning More Converts to the Cause

What must we do to bring more of the healing professions and their clients around to our way of thinking?

We have to change the climate of thinking in respect of individual choices in dying. We have to modify social changes ourselves. Others have done it in universal suffrage, birth control, marriage and divorces, abortion rights, and so on. Here is what I think we must do to start with:

First, be right there on the front line, at the bedside, for dying people who seek our help. Help comes in many different ways, from straightforward advice (which is my speciality), skilled counseling, and supervision of the justifiable suicide of a person who is dying, has fought all they could, and wants a careful release from this world.

The Dutch pioneered this 'at the home' approach from the 1970s onwards, and also the Swiss groups have admirable setups. Non-doctor assisted suicide is often the appropriate action in certain cases. On the West Coast of America, Compassion in Dying successfully launched this type of personal compassion in the early 1900s, and Hemlock's "Caring Friends" began similar work in 1999.

For too long, the Judeo-Christian religions have dominated ethical thinking in the West.

This kind of careful assistance, which comes in a multitude of ways depending on the patient's circumstances, is the most important way to build widespread voter confidence and trust. It takes time and effort but not only is it worth it to be responding to another human's cry for help, it earns admiration from a widening circle.

Religious Taboos Must Be Overcome

Secondly, if we are to eliminate the taboos and fears of abuse that some people have, we must make the subject of hastened death, assisted suicide, voluntary euthanasia—call it what you like—then we must get better integrated into our cultures.

For too long, the Judeo-Christian religions have dominated ethical thinking in the West. I am not learned enough to be sure, but it seems the same position obtains in the Buddhist, Muslim, Hindu, and other religions.

Our goals will only be achieved when there is more written about the subject in an investigative and compassionate way. We need to work for the day when the modern news media will report "right-to-die" matters in a straightforward way and not wait for the "scandal" and "disgrace" incidents which they most love to report.

In sum, we must introduce our subject more healthily into literature, media and the arts so that it is as commonplace to read, watch, or listen to in our lives as watching sporting events or monitoring political news.

We need a few ordinary physicians in different countries to become involved in criminal proceedings: to be the 'guinea pigs' and the causes celebres.

At least we cannot blame Hollywood, the movie industry, for ignoring us. In the last few years there have been four major movies dealing with rational suicide, and all were appropriate and tasteful.

Trouble is, they may run out of material unless concerned new writers emerge.

Existing Laws Must Be Challenged

Thirdly, we need a few ordinary physicians in different countries to become involved in criminal proceedings: to be the "guinea pigs" and the *causes celebres*. If politicians are nervous about our goals, then we should use the courts. But you cannot go to the courts without a defendant willing to take the heat and strain of a high-profile trial. Such martyrs are a rarity.

I give [Jack] Kevorkian the credit for awakening millions of slumbering people to the very existence of assisted deaths.

We need a few doctors who will stand up and say: "My patient was suffering unbearably as he was dying. My patient was rational. I assisted a death on request. I will fight in the courts for my duty to help a patient."

Dr. Jack Kevorkian[1] thought he was the man to shake the American medical profession into changing its attitude on euthanasia. But he failed, and some say did harm to the cause, but others disagree. His public relations problems in respect to enhancing the attitudes to euthanasia were that he was a pathologist and not a general practitioner, and more of a showman than a missionary. More of a media circus performer than a dedicated campaigner. A loner not a team player. He alone thought he could alter the attitudes of the huge American medical profession. He underestimated the respect doctors have for the law of the land. Without law reform accompanying it, they would not take the same chances which he would.

Dr. Kevorkian's final objective was right but his tactics proved to be wrong. But I give Kevorkian the credit for awakening millions of slumbering people to the very existence of assisted deaths.

My plea is for the laws on homicide to be changed to allow somebody accused of a 'mercy killing' to at least plead justification and necessity.

Today he languishes in an American prison, convicted on his own evidence of murder, serving ten years to life. At 76 he may never see liberty again. For all his courage and unswerving dedication, he has paid dearly. His legal advisors are now seeking a clemency deal, and I really hope they succeed. The predicament in thinking about Dr. Kevorkian is that, while legally he was 100 percent guilty of euthanizing Thomas Youk, who was dying, because he video-taped it, is that "murder" in the usual sense of the term?

1. Dr. Jack Kevorkian is a retired pathologist, author and advocate of physician-assisted suicide. Nicknamed "Dr. Death," he helped 130 people commit suicide before being convicted in 1999 in Michigan of second degree murder for assisting Thomas Youk, who was suffering from Lou Gehrig's disease, to commit suicide.

Unfortunately, Anglo-American law makes no distinction on these grounds: "A person cannot ask to be killed." We must get this modified.

The Law Must Accommodate Mercy Killing

My plea is for the laws on homicide to be changed to allow somebody accused of a "mercy killing" to at least plead justification and necessity. Not an automatic, knee-jerk excuse but a factual plea for understanding of the circumstances. Currently no such evidence or witness can be entertained. In my view we should work for a wider interpretation of the laws on death and dying and not just "assisted suicide." . . .

Allow me to make a plea for more honest use of words and phrases throughout our movement. In recent years there has been an obvious backing away from words like "euthanasia" and "assisted suicide" and "mercy killing." I am quite aware that this was done for political correctness, trying not to scare off the politicians and the voters.

But not calling "a spade a spade"—as the English say—is playing into the hands of our opponents, who increasingly are teasing us that we are more sinister than we say we are. Speaking in euphemisms—softened speech—develops into muddled thinking and mistaken actions.

I hope we all here are—as I am—fighting for the ultimate civil liberty, the right to choose to die when we wish and how we wish, no matter what it is called. . . .

Organizations to Contact

American Civil Liberties Union (ACLU)
125 Broad St., 18th Floor., New York, NY 10004
(212) 549-2500
Web site: www.aclu.org

The ACLU is a national organization that works to defend civil rights as guaranteed by the U.S. Constitution. It champions the rights of individuals in right-to-die and euthanasia cases as well as in cases involving other civil rights issues. The ACLU Foundation provides legal defense, research, and education. The organization publishes the quarterly *Civil Liberties* and various pamphlets, books, and position papers.

American Foundation for Suicide Prevention (AFSP)
120 Wall St., 22nd Floor., New York, NY 10005
(888) 333-AFSP • fax: (212) 363-6237
e-mail: inquiry@afsp.org
Web site: www.afsp.org

Formerly known as the American Suicide Foundation, the AFSP supports scientific research on depression and suicide, educates the public and professionals on the recognition and treatment of depressed and suicidal individuals, and provides support programs for those coping with the loss of a loved one to suicide. It opposes the legalization of physician-assisted suicide. The AFSP publishes a policy statement on physician-assisted suicide and the quarterly newsletter *Lifesavers*.

American Life League (ALL)
PO Box 1350, Stafford, VA 22555
(540) 659-4171 • fax: (540) 659-2586
e-mail: eszymkowiak@all.org
Web site: www.all.org

ALL endorses the view that human life is sacred. It works to educate Americans on the dangers of all forms of euthanasia and opposes legislative efforts that would legalize or increase its incidence. It publishes the bimonthly pro-life magazine *Celebrate Life*; the weekly newsletter *Communiqué*; the weekly e-mail alert *Wednesday Stopp Report*; and the *ABAC Quarterly*, a newsletter of the American Bioethics Advisory Commission, a division of the American Life League.

American Society of Law, Medicine, and Ethics (ASLME)
765 Commonwealth Ave., Suite. 1634, Boston, MA 02215
(617) 262-4990 • fax: (617) 437-7596
e-mail: info@aslme.org
Web site: www.aslme.org

ASLME works to provide scholarship, debate, and critical thought to professionals concerned with legal, health care, policy, and ethical issues. It publishes two quarterly journals, the *Journal of Law, Medicine & Ethics* and the *American Journal of Law & Medicine*, both of which are intended to inform health care professionals about issues affecting the practice of medicine.

Compassion and Choices
PO Box 101810, Denver, CO 80250
(800) 247-7421 • fax: (303) 639-1224
e-mail: info@compassionandchoices.org
Web site: www.compassionandchoices.org

Compassion and Choices was formed in January 2005 through the unification of two organizations: Compassion in Dying and End-of-Life Choices (formerly known as the Hemlock Society). This new organization is dedicated to the belief that dying patients should receive information on all end-of-life options, including those that may hasten death. Compassion and Choices provides information on intensive pain management, comfort or hospice care, and humane, effective aid in dying. This group advocates for laws that would make assistance in dying legally available for terminally ill, mentally competent adults. It publishes the quarterly *Compassion and Choices Magazine.*

Death with Dignity National Center
520 SW Sixth Ave., Suite. 1030, Portland, OR 97204
(503) 228-4415 • fax: (503) 228-7454
Web site: www.deathwithdignity.org

The mission of the Death with Dignity National Center is to provide information, education, research, and support for the preservation and implementation of the Oregon Death with Dignity law. It seeks to inform and educate the general public and elected government officials about the Oregon Death with Dignity law, to counteract any attempts by opponents to repeal or limit the law, to advocate for improved care and treatment options for the terminally ill, and to promote the Oregon law as a model for other states.

Dying with Dignity
55 Eglinton Ave. East, Suite. 802, Toronto, ON M4P 1G8 CANADA
(800) 495-6156 • fax: (416) 486-5562
e-mail: info@dyingwithdignity.ca
Web site: www.dyingwithdignity.ca

Dying with Dignity works to improve the quality of dying for all Canadians in accordance with their own wishes, values, and beliefs. It educates Canadians about their right to choose health care options at the end of life, provides counseling and advocacy services to those who request them, and builds public support for voluntary physician-assisted dying. Dying with Dignity publishes a newsletter and maintains an extensive library of death-and-dying–related materials that students may borrow.

Euthanasia Research and Guidance Organization (ERGO)
24829 Norris Ln., Junction City, OR 97448-9559
(541) 998-1873

e-mail: ergo@efn.org
Web site: www.finalexit.org

ERGO provides information and research findings on physician-assisted dying to persons who are terminally or hopelessly ill and wish to end their suffering. Its members counsel dying patients and develop ethical, psychological, and legal guidelines to help them and their physicians make life-ending decisions. The organization's publications include the writings of Derek Humphry, founder of the Hemlock Society.

Human Life International (HLI)
4 Family Life Lane, Front Royal, VA 22630
(800) 549-LIFE • fax: (540) 622-6247
e-mail: hli@hli.org
Web site: www.hli.org

HLI categorically rejects euthanasia and believes assisted suicide is morally unacceptable. It defends the rights of the unborn, the disabled, and those threatened by euthanasia, and it provides education, advocacy, and support services. HLI publishes the monthly newsletters *Special Report* and *Frontlines* as well as online articles on euthanasia.

National Hospice and Palliative Care Organization (NHPCO)
1700 Diagonal Rd., Suite. 625, Alexandria, VA 22314
(703) 837-1500 • fax: (703) 837-1233
Web site: www.nhpco.org

The NHPCO is the largest nonprofit organization representing palliative care programs and professionals in America. It is committed to improving end-of-life care, expanding access to hospice care, and enhancing the quality of life for the terminally ill and their families. Caring Connections is a consumer outreach program of the NHPCO that provides people with free resources on a variety of end-of-life issues, including advance care planning, caregiving, pain issues, financial issues, hospice and palliative care, and state-specific living wills and medical powers of attorney.

National Right to Life Committee (NRLC)
512 Tenth St. NW, Washington, DC 20004
(202) 626-8800
e-mail: nrlc@nrlc.org
Web site: www.nrlc.org

The committee is an activist group that opposes euthanasia and assisted suicide. The NRLC publishes the monthly *NRL News* and the two-part position paper "Why We Shouldn't Legalize Assisting Suicide."

Not Dead Yet (NDY)
7521 Madison St., Forest Park, IL 60130
(708) 209-1500 • fax: (708) 209-1735
e-mail: sndrake@aol.com
Web site: www.notdeadyet.org

NDY is a national grassroots disability rights group that opposes the movement to legalize assisted suicide and euthanasia. It was active in the 1999 fight to put Jack Kevorkian behind bars and in the 2003–2005 fight to save Terri Schiavo. Its Web site contains a full listing of disability rights groups opposed to the legalization of assisted suicide.

Physicians for Compassionate Care Educational Foundation (PCCEF)
PO Box 6042, Portland, OR 97228-6042
(503) 533-8154 • fax: (503) 533-0429
Web site: www.pccef.org

PCCEF is an association of physicians and health care providers dedicated to preserving the traditional relationship between the physician and the patient—a relationship in which the physician's primary job is healing and minimizing pain. It works to educate the profession and the public on the dangers of euthanasia and physician-assisted suicide.

Task Force on Euthanasia and Assisted Suicide
PO Box 760, Steubenville, OH 43952
(740) 282-3810
Web site: www.internationaltaskforce.org

The task force opposes euthanasia, assisted suicide, and policies that threaten the lives of the medically vulnerable. It publishes fact sheets and position papers on euthanasia-related topics in addition to the newsletter *Update*. It analyzes the policies of and legislation concerning medical and social-work organizations and files amicus curiae briefs in major right-to-die cases.

U.S. Conference of Catholic Bishops (USCCB)
3211 Fourth St. NE, Washington, DC 20017-1194
(202) 541-3000
Web site: www.usccb.org

The USCCB is the organized body of Roman Catholic bishops that coordinates, promotes, and carries out official Catholic activities in the United States. The conference is strongly pro-life, and its Web site features articles opposing assisted suicide and euthanasia. It publishes a newsletter, *Life at Risk*, which appears ten times yearly and alerts readers to recent developments in physician-assisted suicide and related issues.

Bibliography

Books

Michael Betzold *Appointment with Doctor Death.* Troy, MI: Momentum Books, 1993.

Paul Chamberlain *Final Wishes: A Cautionary Tale on Death, Dignity and Physician-Assisted Suicide.* Downers Grove, IL: InterVarsity, 2000.

Raphael Cohen-Almagor *Euthanasia in the Netherlands: The Policy and Practice of Mercy Killing.* Boston: Kluwer Academic, 2004.

Ian R. Dowbiggin *A Merciful End: The Euthanasia Movement in Modern Amercia.* New York: Oxford University Press, 2003.

Arthur J. Dyck *Life's Worth: The Case Against Assisted Suicide.* Grand Rapids, MI: Eerdmans, 2002.

Arthur J. Dyck *When Killing Is Wrong: Physician-Assisted Suicide and the Courts.* Cleveland, OH: Pilgrim, 2001.

Linda L. Emanuel *Regulating How We Die: The Ethical, Medical, and Legal Issues Surrounding Physician-Assisted Suicide.* Cambridge, MA: Harvard University Press, 1998.

Kathleen Foley and Herbert Hendin, eds. *The Case Against Assisted Suicide: For the Right to End-of-Life Care.* Baltimore: Johns Hopkins University Press, 2002.

Elaine Fox et al.	*Come Lovely and Soothing Death: The Right to Die Movement in the United States*. Farmington Hills, MI: Gale, 1999.
Derek Humphry	*Final Exit: The Practicalities of Self-Deliverance and Assisted Suicide for the Dying*. Secaucus, NJ: Carol, 1991.
N.D.A. Kemp	*Merciful Release: A History of the British Euthanasia Movement*. New York: Manchester University Press, 2002.
John Keown	*Euthanasia, Ethics, and Public Policy: An Argument Against Legalization*. Cambridge, UK: Cambridge University Press, 2002.
Roger S. Magnusson and Peter H. Ballis	*Angels of Death: Exploring the Euthanasia Underground*. New Haven, CT: Yale University Press, 2002.
Margaret Otlowski	*Voluntary Euthanasia and the Common Law*. New York: Oxford University Press, 2000.
M. Scott Peck	*Denial of the Soul: Spiritual and Medical Perspectives on Euthanasia and Mortality*. New York: Harmony, 1997.
Paul Schotsmans and Tom Meulenbergs	*Euthanasia and Palliative Care in the Low Countries*. Dudley, MA: Peeters, 2005.
Wesley J. Smith	*Culture of Death: The Assault on Medical Ethics in America*. San Francisco: Encounter, 2000.

Wesley J. Smith — *Forced Exit: The Slippery Slope from Assisted Suicide to Legalized Murder.* New York: Times Books, 1997.

William F. Sullivan — *Eye of the Heart: Knowing the Good in the Euthanasia Debate.* Toronto: University of Toronto Press, 2005.

J.C. Willke — *Assisted Suicide and Euthanasia, Past and Present.* Cincinnati, OH: Hayes, 1998.

Leizl L. Van Zyl — *Death and Compassion: A Virtue-Based Approach to Euthanasia.* Burlington, VT: Ashgate, 2000.

Periodicals

Marshall Allen — "Death Wishes: Circuit Court Supports State's Primary Role in Assisted Suicide," *Christianity Today*, August 2004.

Elizabeth M. Arnold — "Factors That Influence Consideration of Hastening Death Among People with Life-Threatening Illnesses," *Health and Social Work*, February 2004.

Desmond Avery — "Assisted Suicide Seekers Turn to Switzerland," *Bulletin of the World Health Organization*, April 2003.

Susan Bell — "Euthanasia—a Wish or Workable Reality?" *Cancer Nursing Practice*, October 2003.

Joyce Frieden — "President's Ethics Council Rejects Assisted Suicide," *Family Practice News*, October 15, 2005.

Michael B. Gill — "A Moral Defense of Oregon's Physician-Assisted Suicide Law," *Mortality*, February 2005.

Linda Greenhouse — "Justices Reject U.S. Bid to Block Assisted Suicide," *New York Times*, January 18, 2006.

Liz Halloran — "Of Life and Death," *U.S. News & World Report*, October 10, 2005.

Bryan Hilliard — "Evaluating the Dissent in *State of Oregon v. Ashcroft*: Implications for the Patient-Physician Relationship and the Democratic Process," *Journal of Law, Medicine & Ethics*, Spring 2005.

Karen Hwang — "Attitudes of Persons with Physical Disabilities Toward Physician-Assisted Death: An Exploratory Assessment of the Vulnerability Argument," *Journal of Disability Policy Studies*, Summer 2005.

John Keown — "The Case of Ms. B: Suicide's Slippery Slope?" *Journal of Medical Ethics*, August 2002.

Edward J. Larson — "Euthanasia in America—Past, Present, and Future: A Review of a Merciful End and Forced Exit," *Michigan Law Review*, May 2004.

Daniel E. Lee — "Physician-Assisted Suicide: A Conservative Critique of Intervention," *Hastings Center Report*, January/February 2003.

Paul K. Longmore — "Policy, Prejudice, and Reality: Two Case Studies of Physician-Assisted Suicide," *Journal of Disability Policy Studies*, Summer 2005.

Michele M. Mathes — "Assisted Suicide and Nursing Ethics," *MedSurg Nursing*, August 2004.

David McKenzie — "Church, State, and Physician-Assisted Suicide," *Journal of Church and State*, Autumn 2004.

Ellen Moskowitz — "The Consensus on Assisted Suicide," *Hastings Center Report*, July/August 2003.

Sherwin B. Nuland — "The Principle of Hope," *New Republic*, May 27, 2002.

Peter Rogatz — "The Positive Virtues of Physician-Assisted Suicide: Physician-Assisted Suicide Is Among the Most Hotly Debated Bioethical Issues of Our Time," *Humanist*, November/December 2001.

Margot Roosevelt — "Choosing Their Time," *Time*, April 4, 2005.

Lawrence Rudden — "Death and the Law," *World and I*, May 2003.

Debra J. Saunders — "Death with Vanity," *San Francisco Chronicle*, January 4, 2005.

Carl E. Schneider "All My Rights," *Hastings Center Report*, July/August 2002.

Judith K. Schwarz "Understanding and Responding to Patients' Requests for Assistance in Dying," *Journal of Nursing Scholarship*, Winter 2003.

Thomas A. Shannon "Killing Them Softly with Kindness: Euthanasia Legislation in the Netherlands," *America*, October 15, 2001.

Bradford W. Short "History 'Lite' in Modern American Bioethics," *Issues in Law & Medicine*, Summer 2003.

Bradford W. Short "More History 'Lite' in Modern American Bioethics," *Issues in Law & Medicine*, Summer 2005.

Peter Steinfels "In the Right-to-Die Debate, the Public Reveals Strong Views, but Also the Ability to Make Distinctions,"*New York Times*, February 11, 2006.

Carl Wellman "A Legal Right to Physician-Assisted Suicide Defended," *Social Theory and Practice*, January 2003.

James L. Werth Jr. "Concerns About Decisions Related to Withholding/Withdrawing Life-Sustaining Treatment and Futility for Persons with Disabilities," *Journal of Disability Policy Studies*, Summer 2005.

Stephen J. Ziegler "Physician-Assisted Suicide and Criminal Prosecution: Are Physicians at Risk?" *Journal of Law, Medicine & Ethics*, Summer 2005.

Index